2007-2009
African American
Scholarship Guide
for Students & Parents

2007-2009
African American
Scholarship Guide
for Students & Parents

Presented By
Dante Lee
CEO Of Diversity City Media

Amber Books
Phoenix
New York   Los Angeles

2007—2009 African American Scholarship Guide for Students & Parents

Presented by DANTE LEE
CEO of DIVERSITY CITY MEDIA

Published by:
Amber Books
A Division of Amber Communications Group, Inc.
1334 East Chandler Boulevard, Suite 5-D67
Phoenix, AZ 85048
Amberbk@aol.com
www.amberbooks.com

Tony Rose, Publisher/Editorial Director   Samuel P. Peabody, Associate Publisher
Yvonne Rose, Associate Publisher/Senior Editor   The Printed Page, Book Design
Jarmell Sims, Editor

Library of Congress Control Number: 2007920232

Dedication

To all students of color who thrive to further their education by overcoming the financial barriers.

Contents

Introduction

Now Is the Time to Apply for Financial Assistance

Congratulations on your decision to further your education! This publication should prove to be a very useful tool to help you find the latest and greatest scholarship opportunities for African American students.

Because personal contact information changes very rapidly, we did not provide contact names or emails (with a few exceptions) for each opportunity. **Instead, we have provided the main telephone number (or address if specified) and the exact web site link, which will lead you to the details that you need for each opportunity.** In rare cases though, a web site link could change as well. If this happens, you should visit google.com or yahoo.com and type in the name of the scholarship, and you should be able to find the new link.

Persistence will help you find the money you need. Confidence in your ability is also important. As with college admittance, a strong academic record and exceptional test scores will get the attention of scholarship judges. However, many other factors are considered, including community service. They are always looking for someone with good grades and proven leadership skills.

Since you want to go to college, you deserve to go. Not only you, but also far too many African Americans, for too many generations have made the sacrifice so that you can achieve. It is time to attain your education and get some financial help.

Start early in your quest for financial aid. It is best to enlist the help of your parents. Experts say that a concerted effort by both you and your parents is most effective. Also check with your guidance counselor for leads on financial aid opportunities. The Internet is also a good source in your financial aid search.

There are three basic types of financial assistance. You may find it necessary to combine these forms of aid:

1. GRANTS AND SCHOLARSHIPS do not have to be repaid.

   $50 billion in scholarship grants and loans is available from federal, state and institutional sources. Billions more are provided by private donors and corporate sources.

2. SELF-HELP college work-study programs in which your university helps you find employment.

   Work-study programs are available to many college students, sometimes as early as their freshman year. Although these programs don't come with a substantial paycheck, they offer you some expense money, experience and training in your chosen field and generally your participation allows you to earn additional college credits.

3. LOANS must be repaid after you graduate.

   An increasingly large percentage of federal aid is available only in the form of loans that have to be paid back. However, keep in mind that an investment in your education—whatever the form of financial aid—is worth it.

Financial assistance can be found in any variety of areas from colleges to fraternal organizations to churches and community groups. Every little bit helps, so continually add to your scholarship dollars with as many sources as you can uncover.

The 2007-2009 BLACK SCHOLARSHIP GUIDE FOR STUDENTS was designed for your success and will help you in your quest to find the perfect match for your interests and capabilities. We suggest that you apply for as many scholarships as possible. Just winning one would make it all worth it!

—Dante Lee and Amber Books

Part One

Preparing For College

Like most college bound students, the preparation for your college education probably began as early as when you were in diapers. Now you are in high school. No matter what has gone on before, you still are at a good point to prepare for and succeed in college.

What Classes Should You Take?

The following classes are musts for you! The better your grades in these classes, the better your chances for college admission and financial aid assistance.

- 4 years of English
- 4 years of math (meaning courses that begin with algebra)
- 2-3 years of history
- 3-4 years of a foreign language
- 2-3 years of science

College Placement Tests: Countdown To College Preparation

You want high scores on both the English and math portions of the SAT, so it is a good idea to take the PSAT as early as your high school sophomore year (10th grade). By taking the PSAT, you can also apply for scholarships, let universities know that you are interested in attending, and discover the skill areas you may need to work on, before you take the SAT.

Here are some great readiness tips for High School Students:

9th Grade:

- Take challenging college preparatory courses.
- Begin researching universities that interest you.
- Begin researching scholarships, grants and other financial aid programs.
- Consider taking the PSAT for practice in October.
- Make community and other positive extracurricular activities a must on your schedule.
- Take a summer course that helps you prepare for college.

10th Grade:

- Continue to take challenging college preparatory courses.
- Continue researching universities and scholarships.
- Now is the time to take the PSAT in October.
- Take the SAT in the summer for practice.
- Broaden your spectrum of community and other positive extra-curricular activities.
- Get a daily planner to help you stay on track and organized with all of your activities. (Make using the planner a habit that you continue through college.)
- Form a study group or get a tutor if you get behind in any course. (This self-help experience can also be used in college.)

- Use the summer to hone your reading skills.
- Get a suggested reading list for college-bound students from you English teacher.

11th Grade:

- Continue to take challenging college preparatory courses.
- Work toward getting as many A's as possible.
- Visit college fairs in your area.
- Narrow your choice of universities to an average of five.
- Begin applying to universities.
- Make plans to visit universities you are considering.
- Begin filling out financial aid applications.
- Start putting your bio together.
- Begin asking for letters of reference.
- Take the SAT in the spring. (If you haven't done so already, take the PSAT in October.)
- Continue to broaden your spectrum of community and other positive extracurricular activities and volunteer work.
- Keep making use of your daily planner.
- Become a pro at taking thorough notes. (You'll need this skill every day in college.)
- Apply early to summer programs at colleges and universities.

What Every High School Senior Should Know:

- **Keep going for A's,** and continue to take challenging courses.

- **Keep attending college fairs in your area.** These events are the next best thing to actually visiting schools.

- **Narrow the application process** to a minimum of three colleges. Watch the deadlines!

- **Finish the financial aid application process.** Watch the deadlines!

- **In October, re-take the SAT if you weren't pleased with your score** and want to do better.

- **You should find out what colleges or universities have accepted you** from March to April. If you have not heard from a college that you really like by May, contact its admissions office to help expedite a decision.

- **Respond to letters immediately.** Your financial aid award letters should begin arriving in the spring.

- **Make sure all information is correct** when your student aid report (SAR) comes in. Then, send your SAR to the universities that have accepted you.

- By the end of May, **you should have finalized your decision** on the college or university you will attend. Reply immediately to any questions or requests the school may have.

- **Take Advanced Placement Examinations** in May if they are offered in your area. Consider taking the College Level Entry Program (CLEP) in an area of study that you are particularly advanced in.

- **Work during the summer** to put away money for your college needs.

- If you are able to graduate early (at the end of the 1st semester of your senior year in high school) work through the winter and spring, perhaps at an area department store, to **put away money for your college needs.**

- **Assemble everything** you will need for going to college— from your study gear to your wardrobe.

- Don't stop your community and volunteer work!

- Consult and update your daily planner at least twice a day.

- One evening in late July, sharpen your culinary skills and fix a dinner (it can be simple) for your family. This will be your way of saying thanks for all of their help and support before you go to college.

- Plan to take a summer orientation session at your university if it is offered. It will help you prepare in numerous ways for your freshman year.

Getting Guidance

Your high school guidance counselor should offer you information and support as you prepare for college. The following is a checklist for topics that should be discussed:

1. Inform students about the SAT, when and where it will be given. Give them a copy of the free "Taking the SAT" booklet, which has a practice test in it.

2. Inform students when the PSAT will be given.

3. Let students know about after-school or evening sessions available for college planning or the SAT.

4. Inform students of the required and recommended courses for graduation and college prep.

5. Share with students college handbooks or guides they can browse or borrow.

6. Suggest how they should arrange their schedule in order to complete courses.

7. Keep students apprised on the deadlines they need to meet.

8. Recommend activities at home or over the summer to prepare for college (i.e. community involvement activities which will stand out on college entrance and financial aid applications).

9. Inform students of the GPAs that colleges require for entrance (and are needed for financial aid consideration).

10. Let students know about college fairs in the area.

11. Review various schools with the students that they may want to consider.

12. Put students in touch with recent graduates attending colleges on their wish list.

13. Inform students of the benefits of a college visit and how best to arrange one.

14. Inform students of the financial aid resources available to them. Share with them any forms or information you have available.

15. Let students know that you will be available to provide them with a letter of recommendation, and let them know what you will require of them in order to write such a letter.

Earn college credits while still in high school!

Check with your high school guidance counselor about Advanced Placement Examinations which offer high school juniors and seniors college-level course work.

Part Two

Top Scholarships/Grants For African American Students

High school students seeking to further their education should embark upon their college years with as little stress as possible. Finding other sources of funding besides the traditional "student loan" will make that transition easier; and for many of those students, it may well make the difference in whether or not they are able to pursue their studies.

The largest source of college financial aid comes from the federal government. Thus it is generally recommended that anyone interested in educational funding should apply for federal aid, with a large portion in the form of a loan.

Around a quarter of a million students benefit from grants and scholarships made by foundations every year. In addition to foundations, there are other types of organizations or groups that provide scholarships; however, their funds are often limited and only made available to specific audiences they serve. These awards can vary from as little as a few hundred dollars to as much as a few thousand dollars.

Expand your options for support, by investigating whether the organizations with which you are already affiliated have funds available. These types of organizations include:

Professional Associations	Many professional associations have their own special scholarship funds to support their own members. Many of these scholarships are for graduate school however.
Clubs and Community Groups/Organizations	An example of clubs includes Boy Scouts and Girl Scouts
Religious Congregations	Religious congregations are a frequent source of scholarship funds and often support students whose families are of the same faith.
Population Specific Organizations	Examples of population specific organizations include The Black Student Fund and the United Negro College Fund.
Corporations/ Employers	Corporations, such as Coca Cola and Microsoft, offer awards for full-time undergraduate students based upon merit.

None of us is entirely independent without connections to any other individual or group. We all "belong" somewhere. Your unique attributes and affiliations are an important factor in determining which scholarships you may quality for. Within the pages of this guide, you will find many resources with emphasis on the Top Scholarships and Grants for African American Students. Use this information to match funding sources with your personal needs in mind.

Accounting Scholarships

American Institute of Certified Public Accountants Scholarships for Minority Accounting Students

This scholarship program provides awards to outstanding minority students to encourage their selection of accounting as a major and their ultimate entry into the profession. These awards are funded by the AICPA Foundation from monies contributed by the AICPA, its members, public accounting firms, and others. The program has been in existence for more than 20 years and has awarded more than $6 million in scholarships. All applicants must be AICPA student affiliate members.

> **Award:** up to $5,000
> **Deadline:** September
> **Contact:** 212-596-6221
> **More Information:** www.aicpa.org/members/div/career/mini/ smas.htm

Arthur Anderson Scholarship Program for Minorities

This program is for African American, Hispanic, or Native American accounting majors. Applicant must display: excellence in academics, leadership, work experience and participation in community activities.

> **Award:** $1,000, $2,500, $5,000 or $7,500
> **Deadline:** January 28
> **Contact:** 312-507-3402
> **More Info:** 666 Third Ave., New York, NY 10017

John L. Carey Accounting Scholarships

This scholarship program provides financial assistance to liberal arts degree holders pursuing graduate studies in accounting. These awards are intended to encourage liberal arts undergraduates to consider professional accounting careers. Applicants must have obtained a liberal arts degree prior to enrolling in a graduate accounting program. Applicants must be liberal arts degree holders of a regionally accredited institution in the United States. Applicants must be accepted into, or in the process of applying to, a graduate program in accounting that will enable them to sit for the CPA Examination at a college or university whose business administration program is accredited by the AACSB.

> **Award:** $5,000
> **Deadline:** April 1
> **Contact:** 212-596-6221
> **More Info:** www.aicpa.org/members/div/career/mini/jlcs.htm

National Association of Black Accountants (NABA) Scholarship Program
NABA offers over 40 national scholarships plus a scholars' retreat. The half-day retreat includes an opening luncheon, followed by an intense, interactive training session in which students are challenged with real-world scenarios in an attempt to prepare tomorrow's business leaders for their introduction into Corporate America. Participants in the Scholar's Retreat are provided travel, accommodations, and a small stipend to attend the Convention.

> **Award:** $500 - $6,000 plus a scholars' retreat
> **Deadline:** only accepted January 1 - January 31
> **Contact:** 301-474-6222
> **More Info:** www.nabainc.org/pages/Student_ScholarshipProgram.jsp

National Society of Accountants
This scholarship is for undergraduate students majoring in accounting. Open to students in 2 or 4-year schools. 4-year school students may apply for their 3rd and 4th year only.

> **Award:** $500 - $1,000
> **Deadline:** March 10
> **Contact:** 703-549-6400
> **More Info:** www.nsacct.org

Actuary

Actuarial Scholarships for Minority Students
This program provides scholarships at the undergraduate or graduate level for certain minority students who are interested in pursuing actuarial careers. There is no specific formula that will guarantee that you will get a scholarship from the SOA/CAS Joint Committee on Minority Recruiting. Scholarships are awarded on the basis of individual merit and financial need and are renewable upon re-application.

> **Award:** $500
> **Deadline:** January 17
> **Contact:** 847-706-3501
> **More Info:** www.beanactuary.org/minority/scholarship.cfm

Society of Actuaries Minority Student Scholarship
Applicants must have taken the SAT or ACT, have a 3.3 GPA, and be majoring in one of the following: insurance, actuarial science, or mathematics.
> **Award:** $2,500
> **Deadline:** May 1
> **Contact:** 630-773-3010
> **More Info:** Scholarship Committee, Society of Actuaries, 500 Park Boulevard, Itasca, IL 60143

Agriculture Scholarships

Booker T. Washington Scholarships
This program is open to graduating high school seniors or high school graduates preparing to enroll in their first year of college education. Applicant must be a minority FFA member interested in pursuing a degree in agriculture.
> **Award:** One $10,000 and three $5,000 scholarships
> **Deadline:** February 15
> **Contact:** 317-802-4321
> **More Info:** www.ffa.org

Architecture Scholarships

American Institute of Architects/ American Architectural Foundation Foundation Minority Disadvantaged Scholarship Program
This scholarship program is for high school seniors, technical school/ community college students transferring to a National Architectural Accrediting Board School of Architecture, or college freshman entering or attending a program leading to a bachelor's or master's degree in architecture. Once eligibility is confirmed, applicant must be nominated by an individual familiar with the student's interest and potential to be an architect.
> **Award:** $500 - $2,500
> **Deadline:** Nominations – December / Applications - mid-January
> **Contact:** 202-626-7511
> **More Info:** www.archfoundation.org

Association for Women in Architecture Scholarship
This scholarship is for females that have completed at least one full year of college course work. Applicants must be majoring, or planning to major, in architecture related field, which includes Interior Design/ Architecture, Environmental Design, or Urban and/or Planning/Design.
> **Award:** $250 - $2,500
> **Deadline:** April 24
> **Contact:** 310-893-7231
> **More Info:** www.awala.org

Arts / Entertainment Scholarships

American Art Therapy Association Cay Drachnik Minorities Fund
This fund is specifically designed for the purchase of books, this fund is available to members of an ethnic minority group who are enrolled in an AATA approved program and who can demonstrate financial need. Note: Students must be active student members of AATA and have been accepted or are attending an ATTA approved graduate art therapy program in order to apply for and to receive a scholarship.
> **Deadline:** June 15
> **Contact:** 888-290-0878
> **More Info:** www.arttherapy.org

Art Majors Scholarship
To request an application for this scholarship, see below.
> **Award:** $500 to $1,500
> **Contact:** Program Coordinator, 200 Deer Run Rd, Sewickley, PA 15143

Arts Scholarship Program
Award offered to a high school student who demonstrates an interest in pursuing an education and/or career in any of the various fields of the arts including the performance of music, drama, dance and the creativity of visual art such as fine art and graphic design.
> **Award:** $1,000
> **Deadline:** February 1
> **Contact:** 949-553-4202
> **More Info:** 666 Third Ave., New York, NY 10017

Arts Recognition and Talent Search Scholarship Program

The Arts Recognition and Talent Search Program (ARTS) offers cash awards, scholarships, and the Presidential Scholars in the Arts Awards for high school seniors and other 17 and 18 year-olds. Students must be studying dance, film and video; music, photography, theater, visual arts, voice and/or writing. During ARTS Week, finalists will participate in master's classes, workshops, interviews, performances and exhibitions. The final judging will take place during this time and a panel of judges will determine cash awards.

  Award: Up to $10,000
  Deadline: October 13th
  Contact: 305-377-1140
  More Info: www.nfaa.org/Disciplines/index.htm

Association of Independent Colleges of Art

This scholarship is for a High School Senior with artistic talent, academic ability, and leadership qualities. Senior must attend an AICA college.

  Award: Contact for details
  Deadline: Contact for details
  Contact: 415-642-8595
  More Info: www.aicad.org

Jazz Club of Sarasota

Applicants must express interest in Art-Jazz dance.

  Award: $10,000
  Deadline: April 1
  Contact: Scholarship Chairperson
  More Info: 1705 Village Green Parkway, Bradenton, FL 34209

John C. Santistevan Memorial Scholarship

High school students accepted in a four-year college, majoring in visual arts.

  Award: Contact for details
  Deadline: Contact for details
  Contact: 800-666-4763
  More Info: www.santistevan.org/johncs.htm

Music Assistance Fund Scholarship

This scholarship is for African American students/musicians pursuing a degree at conservatories, university schools of music or recognized summer programs. Consideration is given to high school students who demonstrate accomplishments and promise. Awards given on completion of application, personal audition, teachers recommendation and financial need.

> **Award:** $500 - $3,500
> **Deadline:** December 1
> **Contact:** 323-877-9100
> **More Info:** www.sphinxcompetition.org

National Association of Negro Musicians, Inc.

Awards are for minority students, ages eighteen to thirty, for instrumental and vocal music. A local branch of the organization must sponsor applicants, who can compete and win local, regional, and national competitions.

> **Award:** $250 to $1,500
> **Deadline:** July 1
> **Contact:** 910-672-1276
> **More Info:** www.nanm.org/Scholarship_competition.htm

National Opera Association Vocal Competition

Contestants must submit a completed application, copy of legal proof of age, a resume photo, required entry fee, and a cassette tape or CD of two arias with appropriate recitatives with piano accompaniment. Finalists are chosen based on the recording submitted. Do not submit mini-disks, videotapes, or recordings with orchestra.

> **Award:** $500 to $2000
> **Deadline:** October
> **Contact:** 806-651-2857
> **More Info:** www.noa.org/voc.htm

Princess Grace Scholarships In Dance, Theater, and Film
The program offers scholarships for theater, dance, and film students; apprenticeships for emerging theater artists at non-profit companies; fellowships for theater and dance at non-profit companies; and fellowship for an individual playwright at New Dramatists. All candidates must be United States citizens or have permanent resident status. Scholarships, apprenticeships and fellowships must be completed in the United States. Actors, directors, set designers, costume designers, lighting designers, and sound designers are eligible.
> **Deadline:** March, April, and June
> **Contact:** 212-317-1470
> **More Info:** www.pgfusa.com/awards/grants/index.html

Corporate Scholarships / Programs

Armstrong World Industries, Inc.
This scholarship is for outstanding African American students named through the National Merit Scholarship Corporation. Must submit PSAT/NMSQT
> **Award:** $2,000, renewable up to 4 years
> **Deadline:** Request applications between August 1 and December 1
> **Contact:** 717-397-0611
> **More Info:** www.armstrong.com

AT&T Engineering Scholarship Program
College seniors pursuing a PhD degree in science discipline may apply for the Cooperative Research Fellowship Program.
> **Award:** Provides living stipend of $13,200 and covers tuition.
> **Deadline:** January 15
> **Contact:** 908-949-2940
> **More Info:** www.lucent.com/contact

Bank of America: Financial Aid Sweepstakes
Apply online or call to receive an application. Bank of America employees and their immediate family members are not eligible.
> **Award:** $1,000
> **Deadline:** No Deadline
> **Contact:** 800-344-8382
> **More Info:** www.bankofamerica.com

Best Buy Scholarship Program
Best Buy is providing over $2.4 million to be given as scholarships to recognize and reward students who have made extraordinary volunteer contributions to their communities. Best Buy is dedicated to encouraging, expanding and rewarding community volunteer service while also applauding and supporting academic excellence. Selection of recipients will be based on solid academic performance and exemplary community service. Consideration may also be given to participation and leadership in school activities and work experience. Financial need is not considered.

> Deadline: February 15
> Contact: Refer to the web site below for details.
> More Info: http://bestbuy.scholarshipamerica.org

Bonner Scholar Program
The Bonner Scholar Program seeks to transform the lives of students at twenty-seven colleges and universities as well as their campuses, local communities, and nation by providing access to education and opportunities to serve.

> Award: $4,000
> Deadline: Varies
> Contact: Refer to the web site below for details.
> More Info: www.bonner.org/foundation/BSP/

Burger King Scholarship Program
> Deadline: Refer to the web site below for details.
> Contact: Refer to the web site below for details.
> More Info: www.sms.scholarshipamerica.org/bkscholars/

Coca-Cola Scholarship Award
This award enhances educational opportunities in the United States through scholarship awards and enrichment programs for young people who demonstrate, through academic excellence and leadership in their communities, a capacity for and commitment to making a difference in the world.

> Award: $4,000 to $20,000
> Deadline: October 31
> Contact: 800-306-2653
> More Info: www.coca-colascholars.org

Coca-Cola Two-Year Colleges Scholarship

Current students, as well as high school seniors, planning to attend a two-year degree granting institution in the fall are eligible to apply for one of 350 one-time $1,000 scholarship award. School officials are asked to carefully consider the eligibility requirements and criteria listed below.

> **Award:** $1,000
> **Deadline:** May 31
> **Contact:** 800-306-2653
> **More Info:** https://www.coca-colascholars.org/cokeWeb/jsp/scholars

Colgate "Bright Smiles, Bright Futures" Minority Scholarship

The Colgate "Bright Smiles, Bright Futures" scholarships are awarded to members of a minority group currently underrepresented in dental hygiene programs.

> **Deadline:** June 1
> **Contact:** American Dental Hygienists' Association Institute for Oral Health , 444 Michigan Avenue, Suite 3400, Chicago, IL 60611

Discover Card Tribute Award Scholarship Program

This scholarship program is sponsored by Discover® Card in cooperation with the American Association of School Administrators (AASA). The scholarship recognizes the achievements of high school juniors in areas beyond academics, and awards scholarships for any type of post-high school education or training. Judging is based on outstanding achievements in areas beyond academics. In addition to meeting the eligibility qualifications, applicants must demonstrate outstanding accomplishments in Special Talents, Leadership, Obstacles Overcome and Community Service.

> **Deadline:** January 31
> **Award:** $2,500 to $25,000
> **Contact:** 866-756-7932
> **More Info:** www.discoverfinancial.com/data/philanthropy/tribute.shtml

Duracell/National Urban League Scholarship

This scholarship is open to minority students focusing in engineering, sales, marketing, finance and business.

> **Award:** $10,000
> **Deadline:** April 15
> **Contact:** 888-839-0467
> **More Info:** http://www.nul.org/scholarships.html

General Electric Foundation Engineering And Business Administration Scholarship Programs

Scholarships are awarded to high-achieving minority students enrolled in a transfer program at two-year colleges with a 3.0 GPA or higher. Applicants must be nominated by college/school official and complete an application.

> More Info: www.ge.com/foundation/grant_initiatives/education/ scholars.html

General Electric LULAC Scholarship

Plan on studying business and/or engineering. Student must have college sophomore status and a 3.0 GPA. Student must also exhibit leadership involvement.

> Award: $5,000
> Deadline: Contact for details
> Contact: 202-833-6130
> More Info: www.csus.edu

General Motors Minority Engineering and Science Scholarship (MES)

Provides financial awards to outstanding minority students enrolled as full-time students in an engineering or science program of interest to General Motors. In addition, summer internships at a General Motors facility may be available to scholarship recipients.

> Deadline: September/October
> Contact: 1-888-377-5233
> More Info: www.gm.com/company/careers/student/stu_scholar.html

Gillette/National Urban League Scholarship for Minority Students

This scholarship is for minority undergraduate students who are in the top 25% of their class and will be entering their junior year. Must be preparing for a career in engineering, sales, marketing, manufacturing operations, finance and business administration. Must be a U.S. Citizen.

> Award: $1,000
> Deadline: January 31
> Contact: 888-839-0467
> More Info: www.nul.org/scholarships.html

Google Anita Borg Memorial Scholarship Program

Scholarships will be awarded based on the strength of candidates' academic background and demonstrated leadership. A group of female undergraduate and graduate student finalists will be chosen from the applicant pool.

Award: $1,000 to $10,000
Deadline: January 15
Email Only: anitaborgscholars@google.com
More Info: www.groups.google.com/anitaborg

Intel Science Talent Search

Since 1942, Science Service has made dreams come true through the Science Talent Search (STS). Intel is the sponsor of this nationwide competition—America's oldest and most highly regarded pre-college science contest. Eligible students include high school seniors in the United States and territories, and American students attending school abroad. Each year, almost 2000 students accept the challenge of completing an entry for the Intel Science Talent Search, with finalists competing for the top prize, a $100,000 scholarship.

Award: $5,000 to $100,000
Deadline: November 15
Contact: 202-785-2255
More Info: www.sciserv.org/sts

Johnson & Johnson Leadership Awards Program

This program is available to minority men and women holding an undergraduate degree in any discipline for graduate study toward an MBA degree at one of seven selected institutions. Selection is based upon exceptional leadership ability and a strong interest in corporate management.

Award: $30,000
Deadline: January 31
Contact: 212-326-1239

Kodak Scholarship and Internship Program

This scholarship and internship is available to students pursuing degrees in engineering, chemistry, polymer science, quantitative business analysis, computer science, marketing, finance, and accounting. Applicants must demonstrate academic excellence and personal leadership.

Award: Varies
Contact: 716-724-7593
More Info: Coordinator, Internship and Scholarship Program, Eastman Kodak Company, Personnel Resources, 343 State St., Rochester, NY 14650

Mercedes Benz "Drive Your Future" Scholarship Program

This year, $1.5 million in scholarship funding will be made available to college-bound students who are the first generation in their families to attend college. Mercedes-Benz USA and dealers nationwide are proud to offer scholarships to students across the country that demonstrate excellence in academic achievement, community service and school activities. Scholarship awards will be granted to students nationwide as well as to students from specific youth organizations.

> **Award:** $10,000 ($2,500 per year for four years)
> **Contact:** 800-367-6372
> **More Info:** www.mbusa.com/drivefuture

Mervyn's Local Hero Scholarship

High school senior demonstrates academic excellence and extracurricular activities. Must be a resident of the following states: AZ, CA, CO, ID, LA, MI, MN, NV, NM, OK, OR, TX, UT, WA

> **Award:** $1,000 - $10,000
> **Deadline:** February 1 – July 31
> **Contact:** Scholars Management Service, CSFA
> **More Info:** 1505 Riverview Road, P.O. Box 297, Peters, MN 56082

Microsoft Computer Science Scholarships

This scholarship is designed to encourage students to pursue studies in computer science and related technical disciplines. Students from across the United States, Canada, and Mexico will be awarded scholarships in recognition of their passion for software, academic excellence, and ability to make a difference in the software industry. We offer four types of technical scholarships to current undergraduate students: General Scholarship, Women's Scholarship, Underrepresented Minority Scholarship, and Scholarships for Students with Disabilities.

> **Award:** Full tuition for 1 year
> **Deadline:** January 15
> **Contact:** College Relations, One Microsoft Way, Redmond, WA 98052-6399
> **More Info:** www.microsoft.com/college/ss_howtoapply.mspx

Northwood Institute Chrysler Corporation Minority Scholarship
Relatives of dealers/employees of Chrysler are ineligible. Applicants must be majoring in automotive industry, have a 3.0 GPA, and show financial need.

> **Award:** $5,000
> **Contact:** 517-832-4279
> **More Info:** Private Donor Scholarship Office, Northwood Institute, 3225 Cook Road, Midland, MI 48640-2398

Pacific Gas & Electric Company
There are two awards a year for four years and four one-time awards. The applicant must be a deserving minority high school senior who has advanced despite economic, cultural, or motivational disadvantages. The applicant must reside or attend school in the Pacific Gas & Electric Company service area. Applications may be obtained from high school guidance counselors.

> **Award:** $1,000
> **Deadline:** November 15
> **Contact:** 415-972-1338
> **More Info:** Pacific Gas & Electric Company, 77 Beale Street, Room F-1500, San Francisco, CA 94106

Prudential Spirit of Community Award
Students must be in grades 5 – 12 in any state. Student must show participation in a volunteer activity that occurred at least partly during the 12 months prior to the date of application. Application must be submitted to a school principal, Girl Scout council executive director, or county 4-H agent by last week in October.

> **Award:** $1,000 - $6,000
> **Deadline:** October 31
> **Contact:** Prudential Spirit of Community Award CSFA
> **More Info:** 1505 Riverview Road, P.O. Box 297, St. Peter, MN 56082

Sears Craftsman Scholarship

This scholarship is available for high school seniors of any age, race, origin or personal belief. Student must have a 3.0 GPA or above and plan on attending a 2 year or 4 year college or trade/technical school

Award: $1,000
Deadline: May 1
Contact: 626-914-4761
More Info: www.nhra.com

State Farm Insurance National Merit Scholarship

These National Merit Scholarships are one-time, non-renewable awards made to high school seniors who qualify as top finalists in the annual National Merit Scholarship Program. The National Merit Scholarship Corporation chooses scholars based on PSAT/ NMSQT scores and other criteria. Achievement Scholarships are awarded to African-American high school seniors selected by the National Merit Scholarship Corporation based on: PSAT/NMSQT scores, Academic distinction, Personal achievement, and Leadership abilities.

Award: $2,500
Contact: 309-766-2311
More Info: www.statefarm.com/about/part_spos/grants/merit.asp

Tylenol Scholarship

Healthcare isn't just a career–it's a calling. Practitioners must dedicate their entire professional lives to helping others stay well. Tylenol believes this selflessness should be rewarded. That's why we have awarded $250,000 in scholarships to students pursuing careers in healthcare.

Award: $1,000 to $5,000
Deadline: September 30
Contact: 877-TYLENOL
More Info: http://scholarship.tylenol.com

Wal-Mart Scholarships

Each year students of all ages and all backgrounds are reaching for their dreams of going to college. The Walton Family Foundation and Wal-Mart Foundation help provide these opportunities through various education initiatives such as the scholarship programs. Last year alone, Wal-Mart and SAM'S CLUB'S gave over $45 million for our company-wide education initiative.

> **Award:** $1,000 to $10,000
> **Deadline:** January 12
> **Contact:** 615-320-3151
> **More Info:** www.walmartfoundation.org

Wells Fargo Collegesteps Scholarship Program

This scholarship program offers 100 high school seniors the chance to win tuition scholarships. All winners are chosen through random drawings. High school students can join the CollegeSTEPS Program to take a definite step in the right direction.

> **Award:** $1,000
> **Deadline:** July 31
> **Contact:** 800-658-3567
> **More Info:** www.wellsfargo.com/collegesteps

Xerox Technical Minority Scholarship Program

Pursuing a career in Technology has its built-in challenges. What need not be a challenge is finding the financial wherewithal that will help you in achieving your goals. To that end, Xerox established the Technical Minority Scholarship Program. In demonstration of our commitment to the academic success of minority students and to the cultivation and recruitment of qualified minority employees in technical fields, scholarships are available (depending on tuition balance on record and academic excellence).

> **Award:** $1,000 to $10,000
> **Deadline:** September 15
> **Contact:** Refer to the web site below for details.
> **More Info:** www.xerox.com/go/xrx/template/009.jsp?view=Feature&
> Xcntry=USA&Xlang=en_US&ed_name=Careers_Technical_Scholarship

Fellowships/Funds/Grants

Alice L. Haltom Educational Fund

This scholarship furthers education in the fields of information and records management. It is supported by contributions from various chapters of the Association of Records Managers and Administrators International (ARMA); companies, individuals, and other organizations.

> Email Only: contact@ahlef.org
> More Info: www.alhef.org

American Association for the Advancement of Science

A Masters or Ph.D. in engineering is required.

> Award: Contact for details
> Deadline: Contact for details
> Contact: 202-326-6400
> More Info: www.aaas.org

American Bar Foundation Fellowship Program (ABF) Summer Research Diversity Fellowships in Law and Social Science for Undergraduate Students

Four summer research fellowships will be awarded each year. Eligible applicants are American citizens and lawful permanent residents including, but not limited to, persons who are African American, Hispanic/Latino, Native American, or Puerto Rican, as well as other individuals who will add diversity to the field of law and social science. The students will work at the American Bar Foundation's offices in Chicago, Illinois for 35 hours a week for a period of 8 weeks.

> Award: $3,500 / 10 weeks
> Deadline: February 1
> Contact: 312-988-6560
> More Info: www.abf-sociolegal.org/sumfel.html

American Geophysical Union

This fellowship is for any students majoring in earth, space, marine science or related fields.

> Award: $42,000 for 12 months plus travel expenses and health insurance
> Deadline: February 1
> Contact: 202-462-6900
> More Info: www.agu.org/sci/congress.fellow.html

American Hotel Foundation Hyatt Hotel Fund of Minority Lodging Management Students

This program is for minority students pursuing an undergraduate degree in hospitality or hotel management on a full-time basis.

Contact: Refer to the web site below for details.

More Info: www.hyatt.com/hyatt/about/diversity/community/hyatt-hotel-fund-for-minority.jsp

American Institute of Certified Public Accountants: Minority Fellowships

Eligible applicants must be a minority that is currently, or will become, a full time student in an accounting doctoral program. The applicant must have a Master's degree and three years of full time experience practicing accounting, and aspiring to become an accounting educator. Recipient must agree to not work full time as a teacher or teaching assistant during this program.

Award: Up to $12,000

Deadline: April 1

Contact: 212-596-6270

More Info: www.aicpa.org/members/div/career/mini/fmds.htm

American Planning Association Fellowship Program

Students must be enrolled in a recognized graduate program and nominated by school.

Award: $2,000 to $5,000

Deadline: May 15

Contact: 202-872-0611

More Info: www.planning.org/institutions/scholarship.htm#1

American Political Science Association Minority Fellows Program

This program is for minority students entering a doctoral program in political science for the first time. Applicants must demonstrate an interest in teaching and have potential for research in political science. Established in 1969 as an effort to increase the number of minority scholars in the discipline, it has designated more than 300 fellows and contributed to the successful completion of doctoral political science programs for over 70 individuals. This year, the Association has refocused and increased its efforts to assist minority students in completing their doctorates by concentrating not only on the recruitment of minorities, but also on the retention of these groups within the profession.

Contact: 202-483-2657

More Info: www.apsanet.org/section_427.cfm

American Psychological Association Minority Fellowship Program
The program aims to increase the knowledge related to ethnic minority mental health through research, and to improve the quality of mental health and substance abuse services delivered to ethnic minority populations. We do this by providing financial support, professional development activities, and professional guidance to students pursuing doctoral degrees in psychology. Applicants should be enrolled full-time in a doctoral program.

    Award: Refer to the web site below for details.
    Deadline: Refer to the web site below for details.
    Contact: 202-336-6127
    More Info: www.apa.org/mfp/hprogram.html

Coro Fellowship in Public Affairs
A bachelor's degree or equivalent work experience, postgraduate experience is desirable. The program is a full time graduate level program in public affairs that offers hands on training in setting the public agenda, experiential learning and making creative and ethical decisions.

    Award: Contact for details
    Deadline: Contact for details
    Contact: 213-623-1234
    More Info: www.coro.org

Fund for American Studies
Preference is given to sophomore and junior undergraduates majoring in Political Science, Economics and Journalism. Annual 8-week summer institute at Georgetown University offering courses, internships, foreign policy lectures, media dialogue series, site briefings and career days.

    Award: Varies
    Deadline: March 31
    Contact: 800-741-6964
    More Info: www.tfas.org

Graduate Equity Fellowship Award

All graduate students, especially from minority groups, as well as the disabled, are eligible for this fellowship. Full time graduate students with graduate degree objectives, residents of California, with a minimum GPA of 3.0 and displaying financial need are welcomed to apply. This award is available throughout the California State University System.

> **Award:** $3,000 (14 awards given)
> **Deadline:** June 1
> **Contact:** 714-278-3125
> **More Info:** www.fullerton.edu

Helen T. Carr Fellowship For HBCU Students

Recognizing the unique role of Historically Black Engineering Colleges (HBEC) in providing technical talent to the nation, the mission is to support and strengthen these institutions as a major resource of African-American engineering graduates. The Committee will work towards the goal of quality engineering education by engaging in programs to increase awareness of the need for African-American PhD's in engineering education and other efforts that will increase the pool of such talent in engineering.

> **Contact:** 202-331-3500
> **More Info:** www.asee.org/resources/fellowships/hbecc.cfm

Institute of Current World Affairs

This fellowship is for students under 36, who know English with varied academic backgrounds. Duration: Minimum of 2 years.

> **Award:** Contact for details
> **Deadline:** Applications available in March
> **Contact:** 603-643-5548
> **More Info:** www.NIGMS.nih.gov

Institute of Industrial Engineers Scholarship and Fellowship Program

IIE's scholarship and fellowship program is in place to recognize under-graduate industrial engineering students for academic excellence and campus leadership. IIE also offers honors and recognition specifically for graduate students, including the Graduate Research Award and the presti-gious Pritsker Doctoral Dissertation Award.

> **Award:** up to $4,000
> **Contact:** 770-449-0460
> **More Info:** www.iienet2.org/Details.aspx?id=857

Jeanette Rankin Foundation Grants For Low-Income Women

Each year the Jeannette Rankin Foundation awards grants to low-- income women who have a vision of how their education will benefit themselves, their families, and their communities. The grants are typically distributed through the financial aid office, but are not restricted to tuition expenses. JRF award money can be used for books, supplies, trans- portation, childcare, or other expenses that will help the recipient achieve her educational goals.

Contact: 706-208-1211
More Info: www.rankinfoundation.org

Minority Leaders Fellowship Program

The Washington Center's Minority Leaders Fellowship Program selects a group of outstanding college students to spend ten weeks in Washington, D.C. Students explore the field of leadership not only as a theoretical concept but also as a daily reality. The president of their college and university must nominate applicants.

Contact: 202-638-4949
More Info: www.fsu.edu/~service/opp/sch_awards/
sch_links.htm#minority.com

National Consortium for Graduate Degrees for Minorities in Engineering & Science, Inc.

The GEM Fellowship programs provide full tuition fees and stipends per academic year for a masters and PhD program. Paid summer internships with Fortune 500 companies. Juniors, seniors and B.S. degree holders can apply. Must be U.S. citizens.

Award: $6,000 - $12,000
Deadline: December 1
Contact: 574-631-7771
More Info: www.gemfellowship.org

National Institute of General Medical Sciences

This fellowship is for minority undergraduate and graduate students who wish to pursue a career in biomedical science. Student must be a U.S. citizen or legal resident.

Award: Contact for details, renewable for up to 5 years
Deadline: February 1, July 1, or October 1
Contact: 301-496-7301
More Info: www.NIGMS.nih.gov

National Medical Fellowships, Inc.

This fellowship is for graduate medical students from various minority groups. Students must be U.S. citizen, 1st or 2nd year medical students and have demonstrated financial need.

>Award: $2,500
>Deadline: August 31
>Contact: 212-714-1007
>More Info: www.nmf-online.org

National Science Foundation Fellowship

This fellowship is for students interested in obtaining a graduate degree in mathematical, physical, engineering, and social sciences. Students must be U.S. citizens.

>Award: $12,300 renewable
>Deadline: November 14
>Contact: 866-241-4300
>More Info: www.orau.org/nsf/nsffel.htm

Peace Scholar Dissertation Fellowship

The Peace Scholar Dissertation Fellowship program is open to doctoral students, regardless of citizenship, enrolled in an accredited college or university in the United States and working on a dissertation related to the peaceful resolution of international conflicts. Applicants must have completed all requirements for the degree, except the dissertation by the commencement of the award. The dissertation fellowship award may be used to support writing or field research. Recipients of the Peace Scholar Dissertation Fellowship award are selected through a rigorous annual competition, for which the selection process begins each January and ends the following May.

>Award: $17,000 for one year
>Contact: 202-457-1700
>More Info: www.usip.org/grants/index.html

29

Porter Physiology Fellowships for Minorities

This fellowship is open to underrepresented ethnic minority applicants who are citizens or permanent residents of the United States and/or its territories. The applicant must have been accepted into or currently be in a graduate program in physiology at the time of the application. Fellowships are awarded for one year, with the possibility of a second year of funding if trainee progress is positively rated by the Committee. Under exceptional circumstances, a third year may be awarded. There is no dependency allowance.

> Award: $18,000
> Deadline: January 15
> Contact: 301-634-7132
> More Info: www.the-aps.org/education/minority_prog/stu_fellows/ porter_phy/about_pp.htm

Registered Nurse Fellowship Program For Ethnic/Racial Minorities

This fellowship program is for careers in behavioral science research. Applicants must be American citizens or permanent residents.

> Deadline: March 1
> Contact: 202-789-1334
> More Info: www.nursingworld.org/emfp/

Roothbert Fund

This fund is for high school students entering college, members of the following faiths: Baptist, Christian, Christian Scientist, Church of Christ, Lutheran, Methodist, Protestant, and Roman Catholic.

> Award: $2,000 to $3,000
> Deadline: January 31
> Contact: The Roothbert Fund, 360 Park Avenue South, 15th Floor, New York, NY 10010
> More Info: www.roothbertfund.org/scholarships.php#fund

Studio Arts Center

Various fellowships and awards to ethnic minorities and women studio artists and photographers to study in Florence.

> Award: $1,000 to $17,000
> Deadline: May 1
> Contact: 800- 344-9186
> More Info: Studio Arts Center, IIE, 809 United Nations Plaza, New York, NY 10017-3580

Summer Undergraduate Research Fellowship in the Department of Pharmacology

This fellowship is open to juniors interested in pursuing a Ph.D. in pharmacology.

Award: $2,000
Deadline: Early April
Contact: 800-743-2782
More Info: www.uci.edu

The Davis-Putter Scholarship Fund

This fund provides grants to students actively working for peace and justice. These need-based scholarships are awarded to those able to do academic work at the university level and who are part of the progressive movement on the campus and in the community. Earlier recipients worked for civil rights, against McCarthyism, and for peace in Vietnam. Recent grantees have been active in the struggle against racism, sexism, homophobia, and other forms of oppression; building the movement for economic justice; and creating peace through international anti-imperialist solidarity.

Award: up to $6,000
Deadline: April 1
Email Only: information@davisputter.org
More Info: www.davisputter.org

The Stan Beck Fellowship

This fellowship was established as a tribute to Stanley D. Beck, a notable scientist who pursued his profession despite the effects of a debilitating disease.

Award: $4,000
Deadline: September 1
Contact: The Stan Beck Fellowship, 9301 Annapolis Road, Lanham, MD 20706
More Info: www.entfdn.org/BECK.html

The William Randolph Hearst Endowed Fellowship For Minority Students

The fellowship, which is based on academic excellence and need, is open to both undergraduate and graduate students who are members of minority groups and are US citizens. The Hearst Fellow serves as an intern with the Fund. Through this program, the Fund seeks to introduce a diverse group of students to issues relating to philanthropy, voluntarism, and nonprofit organizations. A fellowship grant will be awarded, depending on the recipient's educational level, financial need, and time commitment.

    Award: $2,500 to $5,000
    Deadline: December, March, July
    Contact: 202-293-0525
    More Info: www.nonprofitresearch.org/newsletter1530/newsletter_show.htm?doc_id=16318

W.E.B. Dubois Fellowship Program For Criminal Justice Majors

Provides researchers with the opportunity to advance scholarly efforts in research on crime, violence, and the administration of justice in diverse cultural contexts.

    Award: Up to $75,000
    Deadline: February 1
    More Info: www.ojp.usdoj.gov/nij/funding.htm

Zeta Phi Beta Sorority

The Deborah P. Wolfe International Fellowship is awarded to black women for a full academic year of full-time study in the U.S. for a foreign student.

    Award: Varies
    Deadline: February 1
    Contact: Zeta Phi Beta Sorority, 1201 Boynton Avenue, Westfield, NJ 07090

Foundations

Brown Foundation College Scholarships

Applicant must be a minority undergraduate in their junior year attending an institution of higher learning with an academic program in education with at least a 3.0 GPA. The student must be accepted into a teacher education program and enrolled at least half-time.

> **Award:** $500 per year (for junior & senior years)
> **Deadline:** March
> **Contact:** Brown Foundation for Education, Equity and Research
> **More Info:** P.O. Box 4862, Topeka, KS 66604

Business and Professional Women's Foundation

Applicant must be a woman, 25 years of age or older and enrolled in an accredited program. Must be a U.S. citizen.

> **Award:** $2,000
> **Deadline:** April 15
> **Contact:** 202-293-1200, ext 169
> **More Info:** www.bpwusa.org

Coca-Cola Scholars Foundation, Inc.

High school seniors must demonstrate leadership and academic achievement. Applicants must be a U.S. citizen or legal resident planning to attend an accredited university. Applicants must have a minimum GPA of 3.0. Applications can be requested via telephone or through the web page. Applicants whose parents or grandparents are employees of Coca Cola or a Coca Cola bottling plant are ineligible.

> **Award:** $4,000 - $20,000
> **Deadline:** October 31
> **Contact:** 404-237-1300
> **More Info:** www.coca-colasholars.org

Educational Foundation of the National Restaurant Association

For undergraduate students in the food service area.

> **Award:** $2,000
> **Deadline:** April 8
> **Contact:** 800-765-2122
> **More Info:** www.nraef.org

Foundation for Exceptional Children – Stanley E. Jackson Scholarship

Applicants are disabled ethnic minorities with evidence of financial need, and anticipating enrollment for the first time in a full-time post-secondary education or training.

>   **Award:** $1,000
>   **Deadline:** February 1
>   **Contact:** 1110 N. Glebe Road, Suite 300, Arlington, VA 22201
>   **More Info:** www.yesican.sped.org

Future Leaders Program

Applicants must be a sophomore or junior enrolled as a fulltime student in a 4-year university or college in good academic standing and must provide a written narrative (must be a U.S. citizen)

>   **Award:** $1,000, $2,500, $5,000 or $7,500
>   **Deadline:** January 15
>   **Contact:** 301-340-7788
>   **More Info:** www.thephillipsfoundation.org

Karla Scherer Foundation

For women who are interested in pursuing a career in the field of business with emphasis in economics or finance.

>   **Award:** Contact for details
>   **Deadline:** March 1
>   **Contact:** The Karla Scherer Foundation
>   **More Info:** 737 North Michigan Ave., Suite 2330, Chicago, IL 60611

Leopold Shepp Foundation

Undergraduate and graduate full-time students. Must be a U.S. citizen.

>   **Award:** $1,000
>   **Deadline:** Please send a self-addressed stamped envelope to 551 Fifth Ave., Suite 3000, New York, NY 10176 for details.
>   **Contact:** 212-986-3078
>   **More Info:** www.sheppfoundation.org

World Study Foundation Scholarships
This program is open to disadvantaged or minority college students who are currently enrolled at an accredited school and majoring in one of the following areas; advertising, architecture, environmental graphics, fashion design, film/video, fine arts, furniture design, interior design, landscape architecture, new media, photography, surface/textile design, or urban planning. Selection based on a slide portfolio of work, a written statement of purpose, financial need, and a demonstrated commitment to giving back to the community.
> **Award:** Varies
> **Deadline:** March 18
> **Contact:** 212-366-1317
> **More Info:** www.worldstudio.org

General Scholarship Programs

Adelante! U.S. Education Leadership Fund
This fund is for university juniors with a GPA of 3.0 and above. Must be eligible for financial aid, pursuing a business degree (or a related field). Must attend a paid Leadership institute and participate in a business institute. Must provide two letters of recommendation.
> **Award:** varies
> **Deadline:** June
> **Contact:** 210-692-1971
> **More Info:** Teresa Vargas, 8415 Datapoint, Suite 400, San Antonio, TX 78229

Adolescence and Youth Undergraduate Award
This award is for any undergraduate student proposing a research project using Murray Center data is eligible to apply. Proposals must be approved by a supervising facility member before the grant is submitted.
> **Award:** $1,000
> **Deadline:** Varies
> **More Info:** The Henry Murray Research Center, 10 Garden St., Cambridge, MA 02138
> **Contact:** Grants Program Administrator

AGC Education and Research Foundation Undergraduate Scholarship

The Associated General Contractors of America (AGC), the voice of the construction industry, is an organization of qualified construction contractors and industry related companies dedicated to skill, integrity, and responsibility. Undergraduate scholarships are available to college sophomores and juniors enrolled or planning to enroll in a full-time, four or five-year ABET or ACCE accredited construction or civil/construction engineering program.

> **Award:** $2,500 to $7,000
> **Deadline:** November 1
> **Contact:** 703-548-3118
> **More Info:** www2.agc.org/scholarship

American Correctional Association

The Martin Luther King, Jr., Scholarship is awarded to minority nominees enrolled in an undergraduate or graduate criminal justice program in a four-year college; must demonstrate financial need and academic achievement.

> **Award:** $2,000
> **Deadline:** June 1
> **Contact:** 800-222-5646
> **More Info:** Martin Luther King Jr. Scholarship, American Correctional Association, 4380 Forbes Boulevard, Lanham, MD 20706-4322

American Institute of Real Estate Appraisers

The Appraisal Institute Education Trust Scholarship is open to U.S. citizens majoring graduate or undergraduate-in real estate appraisal, land economics, real estate, or allied field; awarded on the basis of academic merit.

> **Award:** $2,000 to $3,000
> **Deadline:** March 15
> **Contact:** 312-335-4136
> **More Info:** www.appraisalinstitute.org/education/downloads/

American Library Association

For students interested in pursuing a career in library and information science. Academic excellence, leadership qualities and evidence of a commitment to a career in librarianship. Applicant must be a U.S. citizen.

> **Award:** Contact for details
> **Deadline:** Contact for details
> **Contact:** 800-545-2433
> **More Info:** www.ala.org

American Planning Association (3 scholarships)

This scholarship is for a minority college sophomore, junior or senior planning to major in Urban planning or a major closely related (environmental science or public administration). Also based on need.

> **Award:** $2,500
> **Deadline:** April 30
> **Contact:** 202-872-0611
> **More Info:** www.planning.org

African Methodist Episcopal Church

Scholarships are available through local congregations. The AME church has over 8,000 congregations worldwide.

> **Award:** Varies
> **Contact:** 202-337-3930
> **More Info:** African Methodist Episcopal Church, 2311 N Street, NW, Washington, DC 20037

African Methodist Episcopal Zion Church

This organization's 1.5 million members, encompassing 2,500 churches, provide scholarships for its college-bound members.

> **Award:** Varies
> **Contact:** 412-242-5842
> **More Info:** African Methodist Episcopal Zion Church, 1200 Windermere Drive, Pittsburgh, PA 15218

Baptist Scholarship

Applicant can be a high school senior, undergraduate, or graduate student that is a member of a National Baptist Convention church. The student must also demonstrate financial need.

    Award: $1,000
    Deadline: Please contact for more information
    Contact: National Baptist Convention USA, Inc., 358 East Blvd. Baton Rouge, LA 70802
    More Info: www.nbcusa.org

Benjamin Gilman International Scholarship

Must be a U.S. citizen enrolled as an undergraduate receiving Federal financial aid. Must intend to participate in a credit-bearing study abroad program.

    Award: $4,000
    Deadline: Contact the Headquarters
    Contact: 713-621-6300
    More Info: www.iie.org/gilman

Call Me MISTER

The "Call Me MISTER" program is a collaboration between Clemson University, private, historically black colleges (Benedict College, Claflin University, and Morris College) and two-year technical colleges to recruit, train, certify and secure employment for African American Males as elementary teachers in the public schools of South Carolina. Students have the option of first attending one of our two-year partner colleges before transferring to one of the four-year institutions to complete their baccalaureate degree. In addition, the project has limited enrollment in the middle school Master of Art in Teaching program.

Procedures for admission to the "Call Me MISTER " program are as follows:

1. Apply for and be accepted into one of the participating colleges or universities at which the degree and teaching certificate will be earned

2. Complete the Call Me MISTER online application

3. Submit the following items:

▲ Two letters of recommendation:

1. one (1) from a teacher, guidance counselor, or principal at the high school from which the diploma is earned.

2. one (1) from a person of the student's choice who can express the student's involvement in the community and/or potential for entering the teaching profession.

▲ An essay entitled, "Why I Want To Teach," which will address the student's motivation for entering the teaching profession and the contributions he hopes to make to the profession and to the community as a teacher

Following the submission of the items above, an interview will be scheduled with prospective program participants to ascertain their potential for teaching and their motivations for participation in the program, as well as to provide an opportunity for clarification of any information submitted through the application process.

Award: 4 Years Free Tuition
Deadline: Request applications between August 1 and December 1
Contact: 1-800-640-2657
More Info: MISTER@clemson.edu www.callmemister.clemson.edu/ ·
Mail: Call Me MISTER, 203 Holtzendorff, Clemson University, Clemson, SC 29634

Caribbean Tourism Organization Scholarship

This scholarship provides opportunities for Caribbean nationals to pursue studies in the areas of tourism, hospitality and language training. The foundation selects individuals who demonstrate high levels of achievement and leadership both within and outside the classroom and who express a strong interest in making a positive contribution to Caribbean tourism. The foundation offers scholarships to individuals wanting to study tourism or hospitality at the Master's (post graduate) level. The foundation also offers study grants to individuals pursuing tourism/hospitality studies.

Award: $2,500 to $20,000
Deadline: April 30
Contact: 246-427-5242
More Info: www.onecaribbean.org/information/categorybrowse.php? categoryid=828

Catholic Negro Scholarship Fund
This fund provides assistance to African Americans pursing a college education. Applicants must demonstrate need.
> More Info: Catholic Negro Scholarship Fund, 73 Chestnut Street, Springfield, MA 01103

CIEE Education Abroad Scholarship Fund For Minority Students
This fund assists minority students who wish to participate in any CIEE educational program, including study, work, voluntary service, and internship program.
> Award: $500 towards CIEE application fee
> Contact: 212-666-4177
> More Info: www.ciee.org/study/scholarships.aspx

Christian Church Disciples Of Christ
Black Scholarship Fund provides Black Americans interested in pursuing a career in the ministry of the Christian Church. Applicants must be members of the Christian Church; demonstrate academic ability, have financial need, be enrolled in an accredited postsecondary institution, and submit a transcript of their academic record.
> Award: Varies
> Contact: Christian Church, 222 S. Downey Avenue, P.O. Box 1986, Indianapolis, IN 46206

CLA Scholarship for Minority Students
This scholarship is for minority graduate students pursuing a master's degree in library and information science at an accredited CA library school.
> Award: $2,500
> Deadline: May 31
> Contact: 916-447-8541
> More Info: www.cla-net.org/html/yelland.html

Coalition of Black Members of The American Lutheran Church
One of this organization's goals is to assist Black students in their total education in college and institutions of the American Lutheran Church.
> Contact: 610-330-3100
> More Info: Coalition of Black Members of the American Lutheran Church, 422 S. 5th Street, Minneapolis, MN 55415

Congressional Black Caucus Spouses Scholarship
Applicants must be residents of a Congressional district represented by a member of the Congressional Black Caucus in Maryland.
> Award: $5,000 to $10,000
> Deadline: March 25
> Contact: 202-675-6730

Cornell University Summer College Program, Jerome H. Holland Scholarships
This scholarship is for Minority high school juniors or seniors who demonstrate outstanding academic ability in addition to financial need.
> Award: Partial scholarships to Cornell University Summer College Program
> Deadline: April 1
> Contact: 607-255-6203
> More Info: www.summercollege.cornell.edu

Do Something BRICK Scholarships Awards
A national scholarship program that honors and funds the efforts of dynamic leaders age 18 and under who have devised and implemented innovative solutions to problems in their local communities in the areas of community building, health, and the environment. Each BRICK winner receives an engraved brick, a higher education scholarship, a grant for continued community work, pro bono services, and other support and recognition.
> Award: up to $25,000
> Deadline: December
> Contact: Refer to the web site below for details.
> More Info: www.dosomething.org/awards/brick/apply

Dorothy Vandercook Peace Scholarship
Applicant must be a high school senior or college freshman with a background in community involvement. The student must also include his/her plan for contributing to a healthy planet, and two letters of recommendation.
> Award: $250 - $500
> Deadline: March 1
> Contact: 530-272-6018
> More Info: www.grandmothersforpeace.org

Ecolab Scholarship Program

Our mission is to provide financial support that enhances the stability, prosperity, and growth of the lodging industry through educational and research programs. Applicants must be enrolled or intend to enroll full-time (at least 12 hours) in a U.S. baccalaureate or associate hospitality degree-granting program for both the upcoming fall and spring semesters. The applicant's school does not have to be affiliated with the Program. Scholarships are awarded for enrollment in two-year and four-year programs.

> **Award:** $1,000 to $2,000
> **Deadline:** June 1
> **Contact:** 202-289-3100
> **More Info:** www.ahlef.org/scholarships_ecolab.asp

Education is Freedom National Scholarship

College scholarships (renewable for 3 years) are awarded to high school seniors with a GPA of 3.0 or higher. Geographic location will be considered in the selection of recipients to insure a broad distribution of awards to all states represented in the applicant pool, provided there are qualified applicants. Minority recipients will be selected in proportion to minority applicants in each minority group provided there are qualified applicants. More than 50,000 students have applied and more than $2.5 million has been awarded to 600 students.

> **Award:** $2,000
> **Deadline:** January 31
> **Contact:** 866-EIF-EDUCATE
> **More Info:** www.educationisfreedom.com

Excellence in Predicting the Future Award

This award is available to encourage students to pursue economics or simply to learn more about the world they live in. The award winners are chosen based on their performance in a contest. Applicants must sign up for a free account on the cenimar.com web site and then use the Cenimar Prediction Market to buy and sell predictions about the future in the same way they might buy and sell corporate stock on a commercial stock market. The prediction market trading is done using play money that is given to applicants for free.

> **Award:** $400 every two months
> **Email Only:** support@cenimar.com
> **More Info:** www.cenimar.com

Foundation For Exceptional Children Scholarships

This scholarship is for disabled; disabled minority; disabled gifted; or, disabled gifted minority students with financial need.

Award: $500 to $1,000
Deadline: February 1
Contact: 703-620-1054
More Info: www.cec.sped.org/student/

Guardian Life Insurance Company of America, Girls Going Places Award

Nominees must be between the ages of 12 through 16. Nominees should demonstrate entrepreneurship and/or financial acumen, have taken the first steps toward financial independence; make a difference in their school, community, or in other people's lives; and show potential for future success. Girls must be nominated by an adult who must submit a 1,000-word or less essay.

Award: 15 awards total: one of $10,000, one of $5,000, one of $3,000 and 12 awards of $1,000 each
Deadline: Contact for details
Contact: 135 West 50th St., New York, NY 10020
More Info: www.glic.com

George M. Brooker Collegiate Scholarship for Minorities, Institute of Real Estate Management Foundation

This scholarship is for graduate and undergraduate minority students entering careers in real estate (and related) and specifically real estate management upon graduation, must have declared a major in real estate or related field, must have completed two courses in real estate or indicate intent to complete such, minimum 3.0 GPA requirement, recommendation letters, themed essay and original transcript.

Award: $1,000 for undergraduates and $2,500 for graduate students
Deadline: March 1
Contact: 312-329-6008
More Info: Brooker Scholarship, 430 North Michigan Ave., Chicago, IL 60611-8775

Girls Going Places Scholarship Program

This annual initiative is designed to help women create, invest and protect wealth by rewarding the enterprising spirits of girls ages 12 to 18. Awards will go to 15 girls who demonstrate budding entrepreneurship; are taking the first steps toward financial independence; and make a difference in their school and communities. Scholarship prizes are awarded among three top winners and 12 finalists each year. Scholarships are presented to each winner and finalist in her community among her peers.

> **Deadline:** February 16
> **Email Only:** diana_acevedo@glic.com
> **More Info:** www.girlsgoingplaces.com

Go On Girl Book Club Scholarships

Go ON Girl is the nation's largest reading group for Black women. Our mission is to encourage the literary pursuits of people of African descent. In this vain, since 1993, we have bestowed our coveted "Author of the Year" award and our "New Author of the Year" award on such talents as Octavia Butler, Gloria Naylor, Valerie Wilson Wesley and Connie Briscoe, just to name a few. We have been fortunate and honored to also sponsor two additional awards, both monetary, to support up and coming authors - "The Unpublished Writer's Award" and "The Aspiring Writers Educational Scholarship".

> **Award:** $500
> **Email Only:** GOGBookClub@goongirl.org
> **More Info:** www.goongirl.org/events/scholarship

Hallie Q. Brown Scholarship

A member of the National Association of Colored Women's Clubs, Inc., must nominate applicant; student must be U.S. citizen with financial need and have applied to an accredited college or university; award is given biannually in even years.

> **Award:** up to $1,000
> **Deadline:** March 31
> **Contact:** Hallie Q. Brown Scholarship Fund, 5805 16th Street. N.W., Washington, DC 20011
> **More Info:** www.nacwc.org/programs/scholarships.php

Harry S. Truman Scholarships

The Truman is a very competitive national scholarship. Each year, the Foundation reviews over 600 applications for our 70 to 75 Scholarships awarded annually. These 600 applications do not include the students who compete on their own campus for one of a school's four nominations. Although the award is competitive, we hope that our application process—while challenging—is straightforward. We hope that by providing clear information to all prospective applicants we enable everyone to produce the best application possible. Eighty awards are given out.

> **Award:** $30,000
> **Deadline:** February
> **Contact:** 202-395-7432
> **More Info:** www.truman.gov/candidates/candidates_list.htm?cat_id=481

HBCU Study Abroad Scholarships

IES is committed to providing opportunities for students of color who have been traditionally under-represented in study abroad programs. As part of this effort, special scholarships and financial aid are available and we encourage all students who qualify to apply for this assistance.

> **Award:** $500 to $2,000
> **Contact:** 800-995-2300
> **More Info:** www.iesabroad.org/IES/Scholarships_and_Aid

HBCU Packard Scholarship /SIT Abroad Scholarships (Study the World)

The HBCU Packard Scholarship has been developed in order to increase the number of minorities who are leaders in the sciences. Applicants must be science majors from Historically Black Colleges and Universities (HBCUs). In addition, applicants must be nominated by a science faculty member. Applicants also must be participating in an SIT Study Abroad program and pursuing a science-oriented Independent Study Project.

> **Award:** $500 to $4,000
> **Deadline:** Varies (by program)
> **Contact:** 888-272-7881
> **More Info:** www.sit.edu/studyabroad/packard_nomination.html

Horatio Alger Scholarship Program

The Horatio Alger Association seeks to assist students who have demonstrated integrity and perseverance in overcoming adversity; strength of character; financial need; a good academic record; commitment to pursue a college education; and a desire to contribute to society. Disbursement information will be sent to you upon the awarding of your scholarship. Scholarship funds may only be used for tuition and fees, on campus room and board, books, and summer school.

> Contact: 703.684.9444
> More Info: www.horatioalger.com/scholarships/apply.cfm

Howard Foundation

This foundation scholarship is for full-time undergraduate or graduate students at a four-year university; priority given to college juniors and seniors. Test scores are required.

> Award: $500 to $3,000
> Contact: Howard Foundation, P.O. Box 5380, Cincinnati, OH 45201

Jacki Tuckfield Memorial Graduate Business Scholarship (for AA students in South Florida)

Student must be an African American United States citizen resident of South Florida, enrolled full-time in a graduate business degree program (master's or doctoral), at a Florida University during the Fall, Winter, Spring, or Summer term of the academic year. The applicant must plan to pursue a professional career in South Florida.

> Award: $1,000
> Deadline: May
> Contact: 305-371-2711
> More Info: www.jackituckfieldorg/

Junior Summer Institute at the Woodrow Wilson School of Public and International Affairs, Princeton University

This opportunity is open to students of color in their junior year of undergraduate study with a strong interest in public service and a career in domestic public policy or international affairs.

> Award: Will fund entire cost of tuition, housing, meals and
> transportation plus $1,000 stipend
> Deadline: November 1
> Contact: Princeton University
> More Info: www.princeton.edu/jsi

Lee Elder Scholarship Fund

The Lee Elder Scholarships are awarded to minorities who show financial need. Also taken into consideration are achievements and career goals.

Contact: Lee Elder Scholarship Fund, 1725 K Street, NW, Suite 1201, Washington, DC 20006

NAACP Roy Wilkins Education Scholarship Program

Awarded to a black student with a 2.5 GPA, letters of recommendation, financial and grade transcripts, and need.

Award: $1,000
Deadline: April 30
Contact: 410-358-8900

National Achievement Scholarship Program for Outstanding Negro Students

This scholarship is for black students who plan to earn a bachelor's degree. PSAT/NMSQT must be taken. Application, transcript, and recommendations required.

Contact: 847-866-0510
More Info: National Achievement Scholarship Program, 1560 Sherman Avenue, Suite 200, Evanston, IL 60201-4897

National Association of Plumbing, Heating, and Cooling Contractors Education Foundation Scholarship

This scholarship is for high school seniors and college freshmen at accredited four-year college; must be sponsored by NAPHCC member in good standing for two years prior to application. Students have to major in Construction Management, Engineering, and Business Management.

Award: $3,000
Deadline: April 1
Contact: National Association of Plumbing, Heating, and Cooling, P.O. Box 6808, Falls Church, VA 22040
More Info: www.naphcc.org

National Black MBA Association, Inc.

MBA scholarships for minority students enrolled in a full-time graduate or doctoral business program.

Award: $3,000 to $10,000
Deadline: March 31
Contact: 312-236-2622

National Black Police Association

NBPA is seeking to enhance higher education opportunities among qualified graduates. It is our desire that through this financial award a student might be afforded the opportunity to have higher educational training in the academics of law enforcement, or other related areas, for the betterment of the Criminal Justice system.

> **Award:** Varies
> **Deadline:** June 1
> **Contact:** 202-457-0563
> **More Info:** www.blackpolice.org

National Scholarship Service and Fund For Minority Students

Awards are based on need and designed to supplement the resources of students who have received other aid.

> **Award:** $200 to $500
> **Contact:** National Scholarship Service and Fund for Minority Students, 322 Eighth Avenue, New York, NY 10001

NAHP – Presidential Classroom Scholars

This scholarship is available for high school juniors and seniors. Must have a 3.8 or above GPA. Interest in Civic Education.

> **Award:** $600
> **Deadline:** April 1
> **Contact:** 800-441-6533
> **More Info:** 119 Oronoco St., Alexandria, VA 22314

National Association of Secondary School Principals – Principal Leadership Award

Student must be nominated by their school principal. This scholarship is based on volunteer work.

> **Award:** $1,000
> **Deadline:** December 6
> **Contact:** 703-860-7344
> **More Info:** www.nassp.org

National Hispanic Scholarship Fund

For high school or full-time community college, four-year college and graduate students who are at least half Hispanic U.S. citizens or permanent residents. Undergrads must have a minimum 2.5 GPA and have completed a minimum 15 semester credits. Awards based on financial need, community involvement and achievement.

> **Award:** $1,000 (renewable)
> **Deadline:** October 15
> **Contact:** 415-445-9930
> **More Info:** www.hsf.net

National Academy of American Scholars

Scholarships are for American high school seniors whom exhibit scholastic excellence, leadership, merit, integrity, and outstanding character.

> **Award:** One annual four-year award $3,000 to $15,000
> **Deadline:** Refer to the web site below for details.
> **Contact:** Refer to the web site below for details.
> **More Info:** www.naas.org/senior.php

National Merit Scholarship Corporation

Students sign up for scholarship by taking the PSAT/NMSQT. Must be high school students enrolling in college or a university the following year. Must be a U.S. citizen.

> **Award:** $2,500
> **Deadline:** October 10
> **Contact:** 847-866-5100
> **More Info:** www.nationalmerit.org

NCR Foundation Minority Scholarship Program

The Paul Laurence Dunbar Memorial Scholarship is for graduating high school seniors or enrolled in a college-level program. Applicants must be studying accounting, finance, business, computer science, engineering, or a related field.

> **Award:** $5,000 to $20,000
> **Contact:** 513- 445-1337
> **More Info:** College Relations Consultant, NCR Corporation
> Headquarters, 1700 S. Patterson Blvd., Dayton, OH 45479

Need Scholarship Program Education Emergency Drive

Only for people of this ethnic and/or cultural background: African American; only for residents of these counties: Allegheny, Armstrong, Beaver, Butler, Washington, Westmoreland.

> **Award:** $100 to $1,000
> **Contact:** Need Scholarship Program Education Emergency Drive, 643 Liberty Ave, 17th FL, Pittsburgh, PA 15222

Negro Education Emergency Drive Need

This scholarship is for black students attending high school in Pennsylvania and accepted at a college in that state. The award is geared toward the average student rather than the top achiever.

> **Award:** $100 to $500
> **Contact:** 412-566-2760

Professional Opportunity Scholarship

Applicants must have completed undergraduate work with assistance from HEOP, EOP SEEK, or College Discovery Opportunity Program. Must major in physical therapy. Financial need required.

> **Award:** up to $5,000
> **Deadline:** June 1
> **Contact:** State Education Department, Cultural Education Center, Empire State Plaza, Albany, NY 12230

Sallie Mae Fund American Dream Scholarship

The Sallie Mae Fund is partnering with the United Negro College Fund to offer scholarships to African American citizens, legal permanent residents or nationals of the United States who are enrolling full-time at an approved institution as defined by Title IV; an eligible, accredited, post-secondary two- or four-year college or university; or vocational or technical school in the United States or Puerto Rico for the approaching Fall Semester. Applicants must meet the Federal Pell Grant eligibility criteria and have a financial need.

> **Award:** $500 to $5,000
> **Deadline:** April 15
> **Contact:** 800-331-2244
> **More Info:** www.thesalliemaefund.org/smfnew/pdf

Selena Brown Book Scholarships

African American college student who has 2.5 GPA. Must demonstrate community service, express interest in researching the black community, be an active NBSW member, and be enrolled for 12 credit hours for the semester before the award is granted.

> **Contact:** Selena Brown Book Scholarship, National Association of Black Social Workers, c/o Scholarship Committee, 8436 W. McNichols Street, Detroit, MI 48221.

Service Leadership Award

This award is for high school seniors and college students who have a minimum 2.8 GPA and have demonstrated a commitment to community service. Must have completed a minimum of 100 hours of voluntary community service in a demographically underserved group in Los Angeles County. A personal statement describing your background, motivation and contribution to community service, as well as your future aspirations will be required.

> **Award:** $1,000
> **Deadline:** May 3
> **Contact:** 323-564-7911
> **More Info:** www.kaiserpermanente.org/locations/California/watts

Special Libraries Association Affirmative Action Scholarship

This scholarship is available to graduating college seniors and master's candidates. Candidates must be a member of a minority group and be enrolled in a library service program. The Affirmative Action Scholarship will be granted only for graduate study in librarianship leading to a master's degree at a recognized school of library or information science.

> **Award:** $6,000
> **Contact:** 703-647-4900
> **Deadline:** October 31
> **More Info:** www.sla.org/content/learn/scholarship/sch-index

Stanley E. Jackson Scholarship For The Handicapped

Applicants must be handicapped and minority students who intend to enroll in full-time postsecondary education or training and who are able to document financial need.

>   **Award:** $1,000
>   **Contact:** 217-244-1004
>   **More Info:** Division of Rehabilitation Education, Chairperson, Science Grant Committee, 1207 South Oak Street, Champaign, IL 61820

Stokes Educational Scholarship Program

The Stokes Educational Scholarship Program (formerly known as the Undergraduate Training Program) was proposed and introduced into legislation in 1986. Its purpose is to facilitate the recruitment of individuals, particularly minority high school students, who have demonstrated skills critical to the NSA (National Security Agency). NSA currently recruits students from all over the country who plan to major in Electrical or Computer Engineering, Computer Science, Math, or Foreign Languages (Arabic, Chinese, Farsi, or Korean).

>   **Deadline:** November 30
>   **Contact:** 410-854-4725
>   **More Info:** www.nsa.gov/careers/students_4.cfm?#stokes

Student Opportunity Scholarships for Ethnic Minority Groups

This scholarship is for minority students with financial need. Applicants must be recommended by counselor designated by the United Presbyterian Church in the U.S.A.

>   **Award:** $100 to $1,400
>   **Contact:** 212-870-2618
>   **More Info:** United Presbyterian Church in the U.S.A., 475 Riverside Drive, Room 430, New York, NY 10115

The Gates Millennium Scholarship Program

Funded by a grant from the Bill & Melinda Gates Foundation, the program was established to provide outstanding low income minority students with an opportunity to complete an undergraduate college education in any discipline area of interest. Continuing scholars may request funding for a graduate degree program in one of the following discipline areas: education, engineering, math and more.

> **Deadline:** January 12
> **Contact:** 877-690-4677
> **More Info:** www.gmsp.org

The Ron Brown Scholar Program

This national program benefits academically-talented, highly motivated Black high school seniors who have demonstrated financial need, social commitment, and leadership potential. The program offers personal attention to each Scholar throughout the academic year. It requires and coordinates career and community-oriented internships. It promotes strong links among the Scholars, and every three years brings the Scholars to a highly-interactive Summer Leadership Conference to promote fellowship and the exchange of ideas.

> **Award:** $10,000 annually for four years
> **Deadline:** January 9
> **Contact:** 434-967-1588
> **More Info:** www.ronbrown.org

The Tillie Golub-Schwartz Memorial Scholarship

Applicant must be a minority and show a commitment to humanity.

> **Award:** $8,000 (over 4 years)
> **Deadline:** March 15
> **Contact:** Scholarship Committee, Golub Corporation, P.O. Box 1074, Schenectady, NY 12301
> **More Info:** www.localstudentfunding.org/content/

53

The U.S.A. Group Scholarship Program

Academics, potential, leadership, and participation in school and community activities are important. A reference is required.

> **Award:** $1,000 to $2,000
> **Deadline:** May 1
> **Contact:** U.S.A. Group, 30 South Meridian, Indianapolis, IN 46204
> **More Info:** www.sonoma.edu/cgi-bin/htsearch

The Women of Color Scholars Award at the University of Pennsylvania

The award provides support to one woman of color in each of these levels of education: undergraduate, graduate and a non-traditional evening school student. To be eligible, applicants must be a woman of color; a US citizen or permanent resident; have completed at least one year at the University of Pennsylvania, or will be entering as a second year graduate student; and be an exceptional student who has demonstrated academic merit and need.

> **Award:** $1,000
> **Contact:** 215-898-5000
> **More Information:** www.upenn.edu/ccp/WOCAP/awards.html

Tri-Delta Undergraduate and Graduate Scholarships

As part of its mission to assist Tri Delta and her members, the Tri Delta Foundation offers undergraduate and graduate scholarships to collegians and alumnae each year. Scholarship criteria include chapter and campus involvement, community service, academic achievement and financial need. Through the generous contributions of Tri Delta members and friends, the Foundation has awarded over $102,000 in undergraduate and graduate scholarships to outstanding Tri Delta recipients.

> **Contact:** 817-633-8001
> **More Info:** www.tridelta.org/foundation/foundation_scholarships.asp

United Methodist Church Ethnic Minority Scholarships

This scholarship is for minority students who are active in the United Methodist Church, recommended by their pastor, enrolled in an accredited college, and in financial need.

Award: $100 to $1,000
Contact: United Methodist Church, Board of Higher Education and Ministry, P.O. Box 871, Nashville, TN 37202

University of Arizona Black Alumni Offering Scholarships

Applicants must demonstrate commitment to the African American community, they must be Arizona residents, they must be legally able to attend the University, students must perform community service on and off campus within the African American community, and the students must be enrolled as a full-time student (minimum 12 units per semester) at the University of Arizona for the academic year for which financial aid is being sought. Applicants must also submit a typed one-page personal statement on the topic: "Has the African American Neighborhood Vanished? What are the Effects of Gentrification?"; a high school and/or college transcript; a completed application and a letter of recommendation to the UABA Black Alumni Scholarship Application.

Award: From $1,000 to Full Tuition
Deadline: Contact for details
Contact: 202-588-8764
More Info: www.arizonaalumni.com/uaba

United Methodist Communication

The Leonard M. Perryman Communication Scholarship is awarded to minority students pursing a career in religious communications.

Award: $2,500
Deadline: February 1
Contact: Nelson Price, United Methodist Communication, Suite 1901, 475 Riverside Drive, New York, NY 10115

United Negro College Fund

Qualified applicants are considered without regard to race, creed, color, or national origin. Individual member colleges where students have applied for admission select scholarship recipients. Applications and selection of recipients are not administered by the United Negro College Fund. (Students must take the SAT test December Exam). The applicants must have 3.0 GPA, be majoring in engineering, and have financial need.

> **Award:** $1,000 to $2,000
> **Contact:** Write for details.
> **More Info:** UNCF, 8260 Willow Oaks Corporate Drive, Fairfax, VA 22031-4511

U.S. Department of Education - The HOPE Scholarship and Lifetime Learning Credits

For students in the first two years of college (or other eligible post-secondary training), taxpayers will be eligible for a tax credit equal to 100% of the first $1,000 of tuition and fees and 50% of the second $1,000 (the amounts are indexed for inflation after 2001). The credit will be available on a per-student basis for net tuition and fees.

> **Award:** $1,500
> **Deadline:** Refer to the web site below for details.
> **Contact:** Refer to the web site below for details.
> **More Info:** www.ed.gov/offices/OPE/PPI/HOPE/index.html

U.S. Department of Education - Upward Bound Program

This program is for high school students who would be first generation college students and/or from low-income families.

> **Award:** Contact for details
> **Deadline:** November
> **Contact:** 202-502-7600

William B. Ruggles Right To Work Scholarship

This scholarship honors the esteemed Texas journalist who coined the phrase "Right to Work" and contributed greatly to the movement's advancement. A scholarship is awarded annually to the student who exemplifies the dedication to principle and high journalistic standards of the late Mr. Ruggles. Applicants are limited to graduate or undergraduate students majoring in journalism or related majors in institutions of higher learning throughout the United States.

    Award: $2,000
    Deadline: December 31
    Contact: 703-321-9606
    More Info: www.nilrr.org/ruggles1.htm

Word Institute of Black Communications, Inc.

Four African American students scholarships will be awarded to black American men and women interested in advertising. Students must have been participants in the American Association of Advertising Agencies' Minority Advertising Intern Program.

    Award: $1,000 to $2,000
    Deadline: May 15
    Contact: World Institute of Black Communications, Inc., 10 Columbus Circle, New York, NY 10019

Government Specific Internships/ Programs/Scholarships

Alfred P. Sloan Foundation

This scholarship is for minority students who have completed their junior year in college and who are interested in government careers. Students must attend accredited summer institute.

    Contact: 212-649-1649
    More Info: www.sloan.org/main.shtml

Congressional Hispanic Caucus Institute, Inc.

Internship. College bound Hispanic high school students as well as undergraduates. Must have a minimum 3.0 GPA. The CHCI also offers a fellowship program for Hispanic graduate students receiving advanced degrees in public policy or policy-related areas. It ranges from aides in congressional offices to assistants in the White House and government agencies and private sector corporations. The institute provides Hispanic students with access to more than fourteen hundred sources of scholarships, fellowship & internships in a broad range of academic fields.

> **Award:** Fellows: $1,550 @ month + paid room and board /
> Interns: $2,000 for 8-week term
> **Deadline:** Contact for details
> **Contact:** 202-543-1771 / 800-367-5273
> **More Info:** www.chci.org

Harold W. Rosenthal Fellowship

This fellowship is for a college senior or graduate student in Political Science, Government Service or Foreign Affairs. The student must be recommended by dean. Fellowship provides an opportunity for a student to spend a summer working in the office of a member of Congress or Executive branch on foreign affairs and government service issues. Selected fellows will also receive preferential treatment for a European community 3-5 week travel study.

> **Award:** $1,800 stipend
> **Deadline:** April
> **Contact:** 2027 Massachusetts Ave., NW Washington, DC 20036
> **More Info:** www.rosenthalfellowship.org

Harry S. Truman Scholarship Foundation

Applicants must be an undergraduate prospective junior in the fields of public service and government. They must have a 3.0 minimum GPA and be a U.S. citizen or legal resident. Preference is given to students planning to attend graduate school and a career in government.

> **Award:** Up to $3,000 senior year; renewable for 4 years. $30,000 total for graduate studies.
> **Deadline:** February 1
> **Contact:** 202-395-4831
> **More Info:** www.truman.gov

Minorities In Government Finance Scholarship

This program is open to upper-division and graduate students who are enrolled full-time and preparing for a career in public finance. Applicants must be members of a minority group, citizens or permanent residents in the United States or Canada, and able to provide a letter of intent from the dean of their school. Selection is based on career plans, academic record, plan of study, letters of recommendation, and grade point average. Financial need is not considered.

> **Award:** $5,000 stipend
> **Deadline:** February 1
> **Contact:** 312-977-9700
> **More Info:** www.gfoa.org

Minority Access Internship Program

This program is designed to allow talented undergraduate and graduate students experience in the diversity and scope of career opportunities available in the federal government and other participating entities. The program provides students with the opportunity to merge academic theory with practical application in the workplace. Minority Access interns receive pre-employment training, expert counseling on career choices, financial management and professional development, and recognition for fulfilling the requirements of the program. **Location:** All States

> **Contact:** 301-779-7100
> **More Info:** www.minorityaccess.org/intern_student_info_04.htm

United States Senate Youth Program

This program is for high school juniors or seniors provided he or she has not previously been a delegate for the program, and is currently serving in an elected capacity in student government. Must be a permanent resident of the U.S. and currently enrolled in a secondary school located in the state in which either one of his or her parents or guardians legally resides.

> **Award:** $5,000
> **Deadline:** October
> **Contact:** 415-543-4057
> **More Info:** www.hearstfdn.org/ussyp

Washington Crossing Foundation
High school students planning a career in government service. Write for complete details. Scholarship Office, 1280 General DeFemoy Road, P.O. Box 17, Washington Crossing, PA 18977

Award: $5,000 - $10,000
Deadline: January 15
Contact: 215-949-8841
More Info: www.qwcf.org

Woodrow Wilson National Fellowship Foundation
These awards are for minority students who have completed their junior year in college and are interested in government careers. Students must attend an accredited summer institute.

Award: $6,000
Contact: The Woodrow Wilson National Fellowship Foundation, 330 Alexander Street, Box 642, Princeton, NJ 08542

Healthcare Scholarships

ADA Endowment and Assistance Fund for Minority Dental Students
Certain minority groups have been identified as being underrepresented in dental school enrollment. At this time, African American, Hispanic and Native American students are eligible to apply for this scholarship. As dentistry's premier philanthropic and charitable organization, the ADA Foundation enhances health by securing contributions and providing grants for sustainable programs in dental research, education, access to care and assistance for dentists and their families in need.

Award: $2,500
Deadline: October 16
Contact: 312-440-2500
More Info: www.ada.org/ada/prod/adaf

AFNA New Access Routes To Professional Careers
This scholarship is primarily for black high school students who have completed the tenth grade and who are residents of Philadelphia. Program is aimed at placing students at medical schools or laboratories to get research experience and earn money for college.

Contact: 215-563-248.
More Info: American Foundation for Negro Affairs, 1700 Market Street, Philadelphia, PA 19103

AHBAI

For high school seniors planning to major in cosmetology, must be enrolled in a four-year college as freshmen, must have a minimum 3.0 GPA, based on financial need.

> **Award:** $250 - $500
> **Deadline:** November 8
> **Contact:** 312-644-6610
> **More Info:** www.proudlady.org/scholar

AMBUCS Scholarship For Physical Therapists

These scholarships are for therapy students in their junior/senior year in a bachelor's degree program, or a graduate program leading to a master's or doctoral degree. Students must be accepted in an accredited program by an appropriate health therapy profession authority in physical therapy, occupational therapy, speech language pathology, and hearing audiology. Awards are based on financial need, US citizenship, and commitment to local community, demonstrated academic accomplishment, character for compassion and integrity, and career objectives.

> **Award:** $500 to $6,000
> **Deadline:** April 15
> **Contact:** 800-838-1845
> **More Info:** www.ambucs.com/scholars/program_information.aspx

American Association of Women Dentists

This award is for a sophomore or junior enrolled in dental school. Based on financial aid.

> **Award:** $2,000
> **Deadline:** August 1
> **Contact:** 800-920-2293
> **More Info:** www.womendentists.org

American Health and Beauty Aids Institute Fred Luster, Sr. Scholarships
This scholarship is for beauty school students. To be eligible, students must have an 85 percent or higher average in school and must have completed a minimum of 300 hours. Extracurricular activities, attendance records and previous competitions/awards will also be taken into consideration. AHBAI established the Fred Luster, Sr. Education foundation in honor of the late Fred Luster, Sr. who was a founding board member of AHBAI and founder of the Chicago-based Luster Products, Inc. To date, the foundation has awarded more than $90,000 in scholarships.
> **Award:** $250 to $500
> **Deadline:** November
> **Contact:** 708-333-8740
> **More Info:** www.ahbai.org/scholar/scholar_new.html

American Nurses Association Baccalaureate Completion Scholarship Program
This program is designed for, but not limited to, minority R.N.s interested in pursuing full-time study toward a baccalaureate degree in nursing. Recipients must be enrolled in an accredited baccalaureate-nursing program.
> **Award:** $2,000
> **Deadline:** January
> **Contact:** 202-651-7246
> **More Info:** www.nsna.org

American Respiratory Care Foundation
Applicants for The Jimmy Young Scholarships Respiratory Care must be U.S. citizens or have visas, be of minority origin, be enrolled in an American Medial Association approved respiratory care program, demonstrate financial need, submit at least two letters of recommendation attesting to worthiness and potential in the field, and submit an original referenced paper on some facet of respiratory care.
> **Award:** $1,000
> **Deadline:** September
> **Contact:** 214-243-2272
> **More Info:** www.arcfoundation.org/awards/undergraduate/young.cfm

Birdell Chew Moore Scholarship

This scholarship is for high school seniors wishing to pursue a degree in Medicine or healthcare. Applicant must have financial need and high academic achievement. This award is for students living in the city of Los Angeles.

Award: Varies
Deadline: Contact for more information
Contact: Watts Health Foundation
More Info: 10300 South Compton Ave., Los Angeles, CA 90002

Breakthrough To Nursing Scholarship

This scholarship is for minority undergraduate students interested in studying for nursing careers. Financial need a requirement.

Award: $1,000 to $2,000
Deadline: January
Contact: 212-581-2211
More Info: http://college.enotes.com/scholarships-loans/foundation-national-student-nurses-association#Breakthrough_to_Nursing_Scholarships_for_Racial_Ethnic_Minorities

Ethnic Minority Bachelor's Scholarships

The candidate must be a registered nurse with a demonstrated interest in and commitment to cancer nursing. The applicant must also be enrolled in an undergraduate nursing degree program at an NLN-accredited school of nursing (the program must have application to oncology nursing), have a current license to practice as a registered nurse, and be of an ethnic minority group.

Award: $2,000
Deadline: January
Contact: 412-921-7373
More Info: www.ons.org

Health Careers Opportunity Program Grants

Assistance is provided for education in health professions and to students with financial need.

Deadline: November
Contact: 301-443-4493
More Info: http://bhpr.hrsa.gov/diversity/hcop/default.htm

63

Health Professionals Scholarship Program
This program is for candidates interested in nursing, nurse anesthesia, occupational therapy, physical therapy, physician assistant training & respiratory therapy. Must be in their third or fourth year of study.
> Award: Tuition, fees, book allowance & stipend paid
> Deadline: Applications available in March
> Contact: 412-921-7373
> More Info: www.ons.org

Indian Health Employees Scholarship Fund, Inc.
For students of Indian decent who wish to pursue education after high school. Must have an interest in a health career and a C average.
> Award: Contact for details
> Deadline: January 1, June 1, October 1
> Contact: 800-279-9777
> More Info: www.nmche.org

Minority Physical Therapist Professional Education Scholarships
Applicants must be enrolled in an accredited bachelor's, master's, or doctoral physical therapist professional education program in California with at least a 3.0 GPA. Students must be African American, Asian/Pacific islander, American Indian or Hispanic/Latino; residents of California; and student members of the American Physical Therapy Association.
> Award: Contact for more information
> Deadline: February
> Contact: 949-824-8262
> More Info: www.ccapta.org

National Student Nurses Association
Nine scholarships will be awarded for undergraduate minority students interested in nursing demonstrating financial need.
> Award: $1,000 to $2,500
> Deadline: February 1
> Contact: 212- 581-2211

National Cancer Institute Comprehensive Minority Biomedical Program

This program is for minority scientists developing careers in cancers research.

> **Award:** Varies
> **Contact:** 303- 497-8717
> **More Info:** NCAR, Human Resources Administrator, P.O. Box 3000, Boulder, CO 80307

National Dental Association Foundation/Colgate-Palmolive Company

Dental assistant, dental hygiene, dentistry and other post doctoral studies, including public health, administration, research, law, etc. for minorities. 2nd year member of Student National Dental Association and first time, full-time dental student. Nomination letter by dean of dental institution, financial transcript and two letters of recommendation, based on academic performance in undergraduate school and service to community. Other restrictions may apply.

> **Award:** Contact for details
> **Deadline:** Contact for details
> **Contact:** 202-588-1244
> **More Info:** www.ndaonline.org

National Heart, Lung, and Blood Institute

Minority School Faculty Development Award program is intended to encourage the development of faculty investigators at minority schools in areas relevant to cardiovascular, pulmonary, and hematological disease and resources. Candidates should be minority school faculty members who are U.S. citizens, non-citizen nationals, or permanent residents, with a doctoral degree or equivalent in a biomedical science.

> **Award:** up to $50,000
> **Deadline:** August
> **Contact:** 301- 496-1724
> **More Info:** http://grants.nih.gov/grants/guide/pa-files/PA-92-073.html

National Pharmaceutical Foundation, Inc. Ethnic Minority Pharmacy Scholarships

Applicants must be U.S. citizens majoring in pharmacy. Submission of ACT, SAT, or CEEB scores required.

> **Award:** $500 to $1,000
> **Contact:** 202-829-5008
> **More Info:** President, National Pharmaceutical Foundation, Inc., 1728 17th Street, NE, Washington, DC 20002, (202) 829-5008

Nurses Educational Funds, Inc.
The Estelle Massey Osborne Scholarship and the M. Elizabeth Carnegie Scholarship. Applicants must be black registered nurses pursuing a masters or doctoral degree program, must attend a National League for Nursing program, and must be members of a professional nursing program.

> **Award:** $2,500 to $10,000
> **Deadline:** February
> **Contact:** 215-582-8820
> **More Info:** www.n-e-f.org/

The AORN Foundation Scholarship For Nursing Students
This scholarship offers financial support to students enrolled in nursing schools and preoperative nurses pursuing bachelors, masters, or doctoral degrees. With the critical nursing shortage and the cost of higher education, the AORN Foundation Board of Trustees knows it is of the utmost importance to fund scholarships for students pursuing careers in nursing and for nurses advancing their professional careers. It is a privilege to be a scholarship award recipient, and nursing students are encouraged to apply for these scholarships.

> **Award:** Tuition, Fees and Books
> **Deadline:** May 1
> **Contact:** 800-755-2676
> **More Info:** www.aorn.org/foundation/scholarships.asp

The National Institutes of Health Minority Biomedical Research Support Program
The Minority Biomedical Research Support Program is aimed toward ensuring ethnic minority groups an equal opportunity to pursue careers in biomedical research. The program provides for academic year and summer salaries and wages for faculty, students, and support personnel needed to conduct a research project. Majors in health science are also eligible.

> **Award:** February
> **Deadline:** Per institution/organization
> **Contact:** 301-496-6745
> **More Info:** www.nigms.nih.gov/Minority/MBRS/IMSDFAQ.htm#6

The National Institutes of Health Research Apprentice Program For Minority High School Students
This program is designed to stimulate interest among minority high school students in science careers and to establish individualized working relationships between these students and active researchers. Apprentices are paid a salary equivalent to the minimum wage.
> Contact: 301- 496-6743

The National Institutes of Health Undergraduate Scholarship Program
This program offers competitive scholarships to students from disadvantaged backgrounds who are committed to careers in biomedical, behavioral, and social science health-related research. The program offers: Scholarship support; Paid research training at the NIH during the summer; Paid employment and training at the NIH after graduation.
> Award: Up to $20,000
> Contact: 888-352-3001
> More Info: www.ugsp.nih.gov/contact_us/

Law Scholarships

Boy Scouts of America
Members present or past, of the Boy Scouts, explorer scouts, or interested in a career in law enforcement.
> Award: $1,000
> Deadline: Contact for details
> Contact: 972-580-2000
> More Info: 1325 W. Walnut Hill Lane, Irving, TX 75038-3096

Justicia en Diversidad Scholarship Fund, Scholarship for high school students interested in Law
High school student must have a cumulative 2.5 GPA on a 4.0 scale. Student must be from a high school in the United States. Must be planning to attend a 4-year U.S. college, full-time next year.
> Award: $5,000
> Deadline: March 25
> Contact: 617-495-4606
> More Info: www.law.harvard.edu/studorgs/alianza

Matt Garcia Memorial Scholarship
This scholarship is open to first year law students.
Award: $1,000 - $5,000
Deadline: June 30
Contact: 213-629-2512
More Info: www.maldef.org

The Earl Warren Legal Training, Inc.
This scholarship is for U.S. citizens who are entering first year of full-time study at an accredited law school, demonstrate interest in civil rights and community service, excellence in academic record, complete application, three letters of recommendation, an essay and demonstration of their unconditional acceptance into a full-time law career.
Award: $3,000
Deadline: March 15
Contact: 212-965-2202
More Info: www.naacpldf.org/scholarships

Thurgood Marshall Scholarship Fund
Merit scholarships are awarded for students attending one of 45 member HBPCU's (historically black public colleges/universities) including five member law schools. Applicants must apply through a campus scholarship coordinator at their school. To date, the Thurgood Marshall Scholarship Fund has awarded more than $50 million in scholarships, capacity building and programmatic support. More than 5,000 Thurgood Marshall Scholars have graduated and are making valuable contributions to science, technology, government, human service, business, education and various communities.
Award: Approx. $2,200 per semester
Contact: 212-573- 8888
More Info: www.thurgoodmarshallfund.org

William Randolph Hearst Endowment scholarship
This scholarship is open to minority first year law students.
Award: $1,000 - $5,000
Deadline: June 30
Contact: 213-629-2512
More Info: www.maldef.org

Media Scholarships

Another Large Production Creative Excellence Scholarship

This scholarship is for college sophomores, juniors and seniors, seeking a degree in marketing and promotions, must submit transcript and brief personal statement.

Award: $5,000
Deadline: May 15
Contact: 310-789-1521
More Info: www.promax.tv/main.asp

Chips Quinn Scholars Program For Journalism Students

This scholarship program is for students of color who are college juniors, seniors, or recent graduates. Students must have a definite interest in print journalism as a career. Award requires paid internship. Scholars are accepted into the program by nomination from journalism faculty and campus media advisers, editors of newspapers or leaders of minority journalism associations. College juniors, seniors or graduates with journalism majors or career goals in newspapers are eligible. Scholar must be nominated.

Deadline: October 16
Contact: 703-284-3934
More Info: www.chipsquinn.org/apply/index.aspx

Ed Bradley Scholarship

This scholarship is for full-time minority undergrads majoring in electronic journalism. Applicants must have least one full year of school remaining and be in good academic standing.

Award: $5,000
Contact: Ed Bradley Scholarship, Radio and Television News Directors Foundation, 1000 Connecticut Avenue., N.W., Suite 615, Washington, DC 20036

Emma L. Bowen Foundation For Minority Interests In Media

This foundation was established by the media industry to increase access to permanent job opportunities for minority students. Students work for a partner company during summers and school breaks; from the end of their junior year in high school, until they graduate from college. Over a five-year period, students learn many aspects of corporate operations and develop company-specific skills. Corporations guide and develop minority students with the option of permanent placement upon completion of their college degree.

> **Deadline:** January 15
> **Contact:** 202-637-4494
> **More Info:** www.emmabowenfoundation.com

Grants for Undergraduates & Graduates in Print and Television Photojournalism

Scholarship awards are given to encourage those who have talent and dedication to photojournalism and who need financial help to continue their studies. These awards are directed toward those who are already studying full time in college or who are returning to college to finish their formal education. One scholarship is reserved exclusively for a photojournalist pursuing an advanced degree. This scholarship program is administered by the National Press Photographers Foundation.

> **Contact:** 828-232-5842
> **More Info:** www.nppa.org/professional_development/students/scholarships

Lagrant Foundation Scholarship

10 scholarships are awarded each year. Scholarships are available for high school seniors and undergraduates who are in public relations, marketing, journalism, or advertising majors.

> **Award:** $2,000
> **Deadline:** March 31
> **Contact:** 323-469-8680
> **More Info:** www.lagrantfoundation.org

MTV University Grants

To be eligible for an MTVU Grant, your project/idea must be: 1) New: This means that the venture as a whole or the specific initiative that the students want funded must not already be in existence. If the program has already been started, it is ineligible. 2) Sustainable: The venture must be sustainable in terms of membership, leadership, and finances. The venture should be created with structures in place so it has the potential to outlast its founders. It should not be a short-term project. 3) Beneficial: The venture must benefit the community; either the student community or the community at large.

Award: $1,000
Email Only: mtvugrants@youthventure.org
More Info: www.mtvu.com/contests/mtvu_grants/details.jhtml

National Association of Black Journalists Minority Scholarship

Open to minority students enrolled in college, majoring in areas of Reporting, Writing, Media Sales, Graphic Arts and Public Relations. Applicants must submit a cover letter, list of honors, extracurricular activities, awards and recommendations from a professor or employer.

Award: $1,000
Deadline: March 31
Contact: 615-259-8000
More Info: www.tennessean.com

National Newspaper Publishers Scholarships

Minority college students who wish to pursue careers in journalism.

Award: $600
Contact: 502- 772-2591
More Info: www.nnpa.org/News/default.asp

Paul Zindel First Novel Award

The award is given annually to the winner(s) of a competition for a work of contemporary or historical fiction set in the United States that reflects the diverse ethnic and cultural heritage of our country. The prize is a book contract on the publisher's standard form, covering world rights— including but not limited to hardcover, paperback, e-book and audio book editions with an advance against royalties and a cash prize. The prize is not redeemable for cash or transferable; and no substitution is allowed.

Contact: 212-633-4400
More Info: www.hyperionbooksforchildren.com/contests.asp#zindel

Radio and Television News Directors Foundation Scholarships

All scholarships are open to enrolled students (freshmen excluded) who are pursuing careers in radio and television news. Winners of the Ed Bradley, Carole Simpson, Lou & Carole Prato Sports Reporting and Mike Reynolds Scholarships also receive an expenses-paid trip to the RTNDA International Conference. Candidates must be a full-time college student whose career objective is electronic journalism, and have at least one full year of college remaining. To receive an award, winners must be officially enrolled in college and be in good standing.

> **Award:** $1,000 to $10,000
> **Deadline:** May 7
> **Contact:** 202-467-5218
> **More Info:** www.rtnda.org/asfi/scholarships/undergrad.shtml

Ruben Salazar Memorial Scholarship

Hispanic undergraduate and graduate students pursuing careers in broadcast, print, and photojournalism. High school seniors are encouraged to apply.

> **Award:** $1,000 - $5,000
> **Deadline:** January 31
> **Contact:** 202-662-7145
> **More Info:** www.nahj.org

San Diego State University

This scholarship is for minority students interested in journalism, advertising, news-editorial, public relations, and radio-TV news.

> **Award:** $1,000
> **Deadline:** April 1
> **Contact:** 619-594-2709
> **More Info:** www.sdsu.edu

Scholastic Art and Writing Awards

These awards are for students enrolled in grades 7-12. More than 600 Art awards and 300 writing awards are presented annually on the national level. Winners may receive cash awards, scholarships, certificates, and publishing and exhibition opportunities. The Scholastic Art & Writing Awards have celebrated 80 years as a unique presence in our nation's classrooms by identifying and documenting outstanding achievement of young artists and writers in the visual and literary arts.

> Award: $1,000 to $10,000
> Contact: 212-343-6100
> More Info: www.scholastic.com/artandwritingawards

SCRIPPS Howard Foundation Scholarships

This scholarship is for students who are in good academic standing, demonstrate an interest in journalism, and have financial need. Request an application during November.

> Award : $500 to $3,000
> Deadline: November
> Contact: 513-977-3030
> More Info: http://foundation.scripps.com/foundation/programs/scholarships/

Student Journalist Impact Award

This award is a concept administered and grant-funded as a collaborative endeavor of the Journalism Education Association and the Kalos Kagathos Foundation. The award recognizes secondary school students who, through the practice of journalism, have made a significant difference in the lives of others. The award program will include one winner with a cash prize of $1,000. Honorable mentions may be given.

> Award: $1,000
> Deadline: March 1
> Contact: 866-532-5532
> More Info: www.jea.org/awards/impact.html

The Editing Program

This program is open to journalists focusing on print media.

> Award: to be announced
> Deadline: February 20
> Contact: 510-891-9202
> More Info: www.maynardje.org

The Freedom Forum
Fifty scholarships are awarded to students pursuing careers in print or broadcast journalism.
> **Award:** $2,500 to $4,000
> **Deadline:** January 31
> **Contact:** 703-528-0800
> **More Info:** http://djnewspaperfund.dowjones.com/fund/

United Methodist Publishing House Merit Scholarship Program
For those interested in employment with United Methodist Church or United Methodist Publishing House.
> **Deadline:** March 15
> **Contact:** 615-340-7344
> **More Info:** Office of Loans and Scholarships, The United Methodist Church Merit Scholarship Program, P.O. Box 871, Nashville, TN 37202-0871

William B. Ruggles Right to Work Scholarship
Scholarships are available for students majoring in journalism. Applicants must submit a 500-word essay, which demonstrates their "Right to Work" principle.
> **Award:** $2,000
> **Deadline:** March 31
> **Contact:** 703-321-9606
> **More Info:** 8001 Braddock Road, Springfield, VA 22160

Military Scholarships

Air Force Society Grant
This grant is for dependent children of either an active duty, deceased, disabled or retired officer from the Air Force. Grant is based on financial aid and a minimum of 2.0 GPA. Sons and daughters of full-time active duty AGR serving as Title 32 and retired reservists with 20 qualifying years are eligible.
> **Award:** $1,500; renewable up to 5 years
> **Deadline:** March 12
> **Contact:** 703-607-3064
> **More Info:** www.afas.org

AMVETS National Headquarters

This scholarship is for high school graduates who are grandchildren, sons or daughters of American living or deceased veterans and are U.S. citizens.

> **Award:** $1,000
> **Deadline:** April 15
> **Contact:** 877-726-8387
> **More Info:** www.amvets.org

Army ROTC Four-Year Scholarship Program

Army ROTC provides college-trained officers for the Army, Army Reserve and Army National Guard. The Army ROTC program is offered at more than 600 colleges and universities throughout the nation. As the largest single source of Army officers, the ROTC program fulfills a vital role in providing mature young men and women for leadership and management positions in an increasingly technical Army. Though the Army is getting smaller, it still needs thousands of new officers each year. The following ROTC's benefits remain intact: training, challenges, excitement, money, career preparation and post-college employment.

> **Deadline:** January 1
> **Email Only:** atccps@usacc.army.mil
> **More Info:** www.rotc.usaac.army.mil/scholarship_HPD2/fouryear/index.htm

Army ROTC Quality Enrichment Program

Participants must be a Black U.S. citizen and be physically fit and have good grades. Participant will be commissioned as an officer after graduation.

> **Award:** $200
> **Deadline:** December
> **Contact:** 513-772-6135

Naval Reserve Officers Training Corps

Applicants must be U.S. citizens and meet age, physical, personal, and educational requirements outlined by NROTC standards.

> **Award:** Full Tuition plus stipend
> **Deadline:** January 30
> **Contact:** 800-NAV-ROTC

Reserve Officers of the United States

This award is for children and grandchildren of R.O.A. members. Must attend or be accepted to a college or university.

> **Award:** $500
> **Deadline:** April 10
> **Contact:** 202-479-2200
> **More Info:** Memorial Scholarship Fund, One Constitution Ave., NE Washington, DC 20002

United States Air Force ROTC 4-Year Scholarship Program

Students at least 17 years old, interested in the fields of aeronautics, aerospace, astronautical science, civil engineering, mechanical engineering, mathematics or physics. Award can be used at any campus that offers Air Force ROTC.

> **Award:** Contact for details
> **Deadline:** Contact for details
> **Contact:** 866-423-7682
> **More Info:** www.afrotc.com/home.htm

United States Army Emergency Relief Scholarship

This scholarship is for unmarried dependent children of members of the army. Must be a U.S. citizen and not yet 22 years of age on June 1st of the school year that begins the following September.

> **Award:** $2,000
> **Deadline:** March 1
> **Contact:** 703-428-0000
> **More Info:** www.aerhq.org/ArmyEmergencyRelief.htm

United States Marine Corps Scholarship Foundation

This scholarship is for children of U.S. Marines or dependent children of former Marines. Must be used for undergraduate or vocational study.

> **Award:** $500 - $2,500; renewable for 4 years
> **Deadline:** April 15
> **Contact:** 800-292-7777
> **More Info:** www.marine-scholars.org

Science / Technology

Ace Ventures Web Design Scholarship

Ace Ventures Inc., is offering first and second prize scholarships to any college or high school student. The money can be used for tuition, books, or room and board. The contest is to see who can create the two best car enthusiast web sites. We are looking for web sites that are up to par with vwvortex.com to be considered. The person that designs the best web site chosen will receive a scholarship, we will purchase the domain name for you, and your site will be hosted on our server with a statement that you won the contest.

> **Award:** $250 to $500
> **Deadline:** After 500 submissions
> **Contact:** 650-347-0445
> **More Info:** www.acecarparts.com/scholarship.html

AHBAI

For high school seniors planning to major in chemistry, business or engineering, must be enrolled in a four-year college as freshmen, must have a minimum 3.0 GPA, based on financial need.

> **Award:** $250 - $500
> **Deadline:** April 15
> **Contact:** 312-644-6610
> **More Info:** www.aerhq.org/ArmyEmergencyRelief.htm

Al-Ben Scholarship

This scholarship is for African American high school seniors, high school graduates, or college students from LA area or currently attending an institution of higher learning and interested in majoring in the sciences or engineering.

> **Award:** Contact for details
> **Deadline:** January
> **Contact:** Los Angeles Council of Black Professional Engineers
> **More Info:** 4401 Crenshaw Boulevard, Los Angeles, CA 90043

American Chemical Society/Minority Scholars Program

This program is a CATALYST for African American, Hispanic/Latino and American Indian students seeking to pursue undergraduate college degrees in chemical sciences and chemical technology. To be considered a candidate, students should meet the following criteria:

1 African-American, Hispanic/Latino, or American Indian;

2 U.S. citizen or permanent resident of the U.S.;

3 A full-time student at an accredited college, university, or community college;

4 High academic achievers in chemistry or science (Grade Point Average 3.0, "B" or better);

5 Able to demonstrate evidence of financial need according to FAFSA form (Free Application for Federal Student Aid) and the Student Aid Report (SAR) form;

6 A graduating high school senior, college freshman, sophomore or junior intending to or already majoring in chemistry, biochemistry, chemical engineering or a chemically-related science and planning a career in the chemical sciences or chemical technology;

*Please note that students intending to enter pre-med programs or pursing a degree in pharmacy are not eligible for this scholarship.

    Award: $2,500 to $5,000
    Deadline: March
    Contact: 800-227-5558 (Ext. 6250)
    More Info: www.chemistry.org

American Consulting Engineers Council Scholarship Program

This scholarship program is for undergraduate juniors, seniors and fifth year students enrolled in a college accredited by the Board of Engineering and Technology. U.S. citizen.

    Award: $1,000 - $5,000
    Deadline: Contact for details
    Contact: 202-347-7474
    More Info: www.acec.org

American Geological Institute, Minority Participation

Students are judged on academic achievement, financial need, and potential for success. Students must be a U.S. citizen and majoring in one of the following: geology, meteorology, geochemistry, planetary geology, geophysics, oceanography, hydrology, or earth sciences.

Award: $500 to $3,000
Deadline: March 1
Contact: 713-789-9525
More Info: www.agiweb.org/mpp/

American Meteorological Society

This scholarship is for any minority students attending or planning to attend a four-year college full-time. The scholarship is based on academic achievement, recommendations, SAT/ACT or GRE test scores.

Award: $3,000
Deadline: February 9
Contact: American Meteorological Society, 45 Beacon Street, Boston, MA 02108
More Info: www.ametsoc.org/amsstudentinfo/scholfeldocs/index.html

American Nuclear Society (ANS) Undergraduate Scholarships

To be eligible, student must have completed a minimum of two academic years in a four-year nuclear engineering program, and must be a U.S. citizen or permanent resident.

Award: $1,000 - $4,000
Deadline: February 1
Contact: 708-352-6611
More Info: www.ans.org

American Physical Society

The APS Minorities Scholarship Program is for minority high school seniors or college freshmen and sophomores majoring in physics. Applicants must complete application and personal statements as well as provide references, official transcripts, and standardized test scores.

Award: $500 to $3,000
Deadline: February 1
Contact: 301-209-3232
More Info: www.aps.org/programs/minorities/honors/scholarship

American Society of Civil Engineers

This scholarship is for undergraduate freshmen or juniors pursuing a degree in engineering.

Award: $2,000
Deadline: January
Contact: 800-548-2723
More Info: www.asce.org

American Society of Safety Engineers (ASSE) Foundation Scholarship Awards

These scholarships are available to full-time minority students pursuing an undergraduate degree in occupational safety, health, or environment. Applicants must be a U.S. citizen and have a minimum 3.25 GPA. A recommendation by a safety faculty member is required. ASSE is the oldest and largest professional safety organization. Its members manage, supervise and consult on safety, health, and environmental issues in industry, insurance, government and education.

Award: $1,000
Deadline: December 1
More Info: www.asse.org/foundat.htm

American Society for Microbiology

Applicant must be a minority undergraduate that has taken introduction courses in biology or chemistry. The student must not be graduating before the conclusion of the program in the summer. Further preferred criteria include lab research experience, and an interest in obtaining a doctorate degree.

Award: $4,500 for expenses
Deadline: February 1
Contact: 202-942-9283
More Info: www.asm.org/edusrc/edu23b.htm

Anchor Environmental Scholarship

Anchor Environmental is an environmental science and engineering consulting firm whose expertise and focus is in aquatic-based remediation and waterfront development projects. To promote and help support those who have chosen these fields of study, Anchor has established a scholarship fund to assist graduate students in their pursuit of higher education. Individual scholarship awards will be provided to the recipient's institution of higher learning to be disbursed to the student for graduate school tuition and supplies.

Award: $500 to $5,000
Deadline: November
Email Only: scholarship@anchorenv.com
More Info: www.anchorenv.com/Scholarship.htm

Anderson Consulting Scholarship Program for Minorities

This scholarship is open to African Americans, Hispanic Americans and Native Americans who are enrolled in their third year of undergraduate study. Applicants must have a 3.0 GPA and be majoring in engineering, computer science, information systems (including accounting, business, computer, management and related fields), or decision or management sciences. US citizenship is required although asylees and refugees are also eligible to apply.

Award: $2,500
Deadline: January
Contact: 507-931-1682
More Info: 1505 Riverview Road, P.O. Box 297, St. Peter, MN 56082

ASHRAE Engineering Scholarship Program

This program is designed to encourage and assist heating, ventilating, air conditioning and refrigeration (HVAC&R) education through its granting of scholarships and fellowships. The program also serves the public interest by aiding in the education of men and women to become qualified to practice as engineers in the HVAC&R field. Scholarships are available to undergraduate engineering, engineering technology and graduate students enrolled full-time in a curriculum approved by the Accreditation Board for Engineering and Technology (ABET).

Award: $3,000 to $10,000
Deadline: December 1
Contact: 404-636-8400
More Info: www.ashrae.org/students/page/747

AT&T Bell Laboratories Engineering Scholarships
Applicants must be minority students with a 3.0 GPA majoring in electrical or mechanical engineering or computer science.
> Deadline: January 15
> Contact: 908-949-294
> More Info: AT&T Bell Laboratories, University Relations, 600 Mountain Ave., Room 3D 304, Murray Hill NJ 7974

Development Fund for Black Students in Science and Technology
This endowment fund provides scholarships to African-American undergraduate students who enroll in scientific or technical fields of study at Historically Black Colleges and Universities (HBCUs). The amount of the scholarships awarded each student is determined by either the National Merit Negro Achievement Scholarship Program or by the DFBSST Independent Scholarship Committee. Scholarships are based on merit and financial need. Applications can be obtained by contacting the science or engineering department of one of the schools listed. We do not distribute applications directly to students.
> Award: $2,000
> Deadline: June 15
> Contact: 202-635-3604
> More Info: http://ourworld.compuserve.com/homepages/dlhinson

Earthwatch Expeditions Inc.
This scholarship is for high school students interested in the fields of archaeology, anthropology, environmental studies, biology, or marine science. Recipients are given the opportunity to work in the field 2-3 weeks with a professional scientist on a research expedition.
> Award: Contact for details
> Deadline: March 15
> Contact: 978-461-0081
> More Info: www.earthwatch.org/ed/scdurfee.html

Ethan and Allan Murphy Memorial Scholarship
Candidates must be entering their final undergraduate year and majoring in meteorology or some aspect of the atmospheric, or related oceanic and hydrologic sciences. Applicants must be U.S. citizens or permanent residents enrolled full time at an accredited U.S. institution, and have a cumulative GPA of at least 3.0.

> **Award:** $2,000 for expenses
> **Deadline:** February
> **Contact:** 617-227-2426
> **More Info:** www.asm.org/edusrc/edu23b.htm

Equal Opportunity Publications Scholarship Program
Applicants must be a full time female student working toward a bachelor's degree in any engineering discipline. Selection based on GPA, extracurricular activities, a personal statement, and a recommendation only.

> **Award:** $50
> **Deadline:** February 15
> **Contact:** 609-795-9634

Explorers Club Youth Activity Grant
The Youth Activity Grant is available to full-time high school students and undergraduate college students to enable them to participate in field research in the natural sciences under the supervision of a qualified scientist and/or institution. In addition to the application applicants must submit a three-page explanation of their proposed project and two letters of recommendation to be eligible for this award.

> **Award:** $500 - $1,500
> **Deadline:** January
> **More Info:** www.explorers.org/resources/funding/youthfund

Flipnut Innovations General Education Scholarship

Flipnut Innovations offers a semi-annual scholarship for any student planning to pursue a career in Information Technology (also called Information Systems or Computer Science). Information Technology is a rewarding career path to pursue, and this scholarship is to help offset the costs of getting a good education from a solid higher-learning institution. Shortly after the deadline, we will choose a recipient and send information about the winner.

> **Award:** $500 twice per year
> **Deadline:** June 30 and December 31
> **Contact:** Refer to the web site below for details.
> **More Info:** www.flipnut.com/general/apply.php

Minority Geoscience Undergraduate Scholarships

Applicants must be geoscience majors (or a related field) who are U.S. citizens and members of the following underrepresented ethnic minority groups: African Americans, Hispanics, and Native Americans (American Indians, Eskimos, Hawaiians and Samoans). Related geoscience fields include geology, hydrology, meteorology, physical oceanography, planetary, geology, and earth science education.

> **Award:** up to $10,500
> **Deadline:** January
> **Contact:** 703-379-2480
> **More Info:** www.agiweb.org

Minority Scholars

African American, Hispanic/Latino, American Indian, Alaskan Native and native pacific islander who is a freshman to senior student in a four or two year university. Applicants must be pursuing degree in chemistry, biochemistry, chemical engineering or related chemical science fields such as material science, toxicology and environmental science.

> **Award:** $1,500
> **Deadline:** Contact for details
> **Contact:** 800-227-5558
> **More Info:** American Chemicals Society Minority Scholars, 1156 16th St. NW, Washington, DC 20036

NAACP Scholarship Program

Applicants must be members of the NAACP who are majoring in the fields of engineering, science, computer science, mathematics, or environmental science. Applicants must be U.S. citizens and enrolled or accepted at an accredited college or university in the U.S. and must be graduating high school seniors who rank in the top third of their class with a 3.0 GPA.

Award: $1,000 to $5,000
Deadline: April 30
Contact: 410-486-9135
More Info: www.naacp.org/advocacy/education/

NAACP Willems Scholarship

The Willems Scholarship is awarded to a black U.S. citizen with a 3.0 GPA. Applicants must be majoring in mathematics, physics, engineering, or chemistry and be active in the NAACP.

Award: $2,000 to $3,000
Contact: 401-358-8900
More Info: www.naacp.org/advocacy/education/

NACME Scholarship

NACME is widely known as the nation's largest private source of scholarships for African American, American Indian and Latino women and men in engineering. Over 15 percent of all minority engineering graduates since 1974 have received scholarship support from NACME and are now leaders in government, industry and academia.

Award: $500 - $3,000
Deadline: Open
Contact: 800-888-9929
More Info: www.racme.org

National Science Teachers Association

This award is for high school students who create and build an original working device powered by one or more Duracell batteries. Must be a U.S. citizen or a legal resident.

Award: $1,000
Deadline: February 1
Contact: 703-243-7100
More Info: www.nsta.org

National Security Agency Undergraduate Training Program

This program is for any student, particularly a minority student, who chooses a full-time college major in electrical or computer engineering, computer science, mathematics, or Asian, Middle Eastern, or Slavic languages. Students must maintain a 3.0 GPA. After graduation, the student must work for NSA for at least one and half times the length of study.

> **Award:** Full tuition
> **Deadline:** November 30
> **Contact:** 800-669-0703
> **More Info:** www.adventuresineducation.org/Scholarships

National Society of Black Engineers Scholarships

NSBE provides various scholarships to our members through our NSBE and Corporate Scholarship Programs. In 2004, we introduced a new NSBE Scholarship Program that merges our former Member of the Year Program and the Distinguished Fellow Program. This award is the highest honor a NSBE member at the collegiate or graduate level can receive and includes a scholarship.

> **Award:** $500 to $15,000
> **Deadline:** January 17
> **Contact:** 703-549-2207
> **More Info:** www.nsbe.org/scholarships

National Society of Professional Engineers Racial Minority Grants

This grant is for minority females who are high school seniors who rank in the top quarter of their class, with plans to major in engineering. Financial need required.

> **Award:** $1,000
> **Contact:** 202-463-2300

National Space Club Goddard Scholarship

This scholarship is for undergraduate juniors and seniors who plan to specialize in aerospace science and technology (must be a US citizen).

> **Award:** $10,000
> **Deadline:** January 8
> **Contact:** 202-973-8661

National Technical Association

This award is for minority students pursuing degrees in finance and engineering.

Award: 50% tuition
Deadline: March 31
Contact: 202-829-6100

National Urban League

The Dart & Kraft/National Urban League Scholarship is awarded to minorities in good scholastic standing. Applicants must be full-time undergraduate juniors pursuing bachelor's degrees in engineering, marketing, manufacturing operations, finance, or business adminis-tration at an accredited institution.

Award: $1,000 to $10,000
Deadline: April
Contact: 212-310-9000

NIAID Minority Research Enhancement Award

The National Institute of Allergy and Infectious Diseases provide support for underrepresented minority researchers. Candidates must be majoring in biomedical research.

Contact: 301-496-3461

Society of Exploration Geophysics

This award is for entering freshmen and undergraduate students in financial need who maintain above average grades. Students should be pursuing a career in geophysics, physics, mathematics and/or geology.

Award: $500 - $3,000
Deadline: March 1 - September
Contact: 918-497-5574
More Info: www.seg.org

Society of Women Engineers

These scholarships are targeted for women who are majoring in engineering or computer science.

Award: $2,000 to $5,000
Deadline: May 15
Email Only: scholarshipapplication@swe.org
More Info: www.swe.org/

Sororities / Fraternities

Alpha Kappa Alpha Educational Advancement Scholarship

Unmet financial need scholarships are awarded to students who, in addition to good academic standing, need financial assistance in order to complete a particular program of study. To be eligible for a merit scholarship, the applicant must have completed a minimum of one year in a degree granting institution; be continuing a program of education in such an institution; demonstrate exceptional academic achievement, as evidenced by a GPA of 3.0 or higher; and show evidence of leadership by participation in community or campus activities.

> **Award:** $750 to $1,500
> **Deadline:** January 15
> **Contact:** Refer to the web site below for details.
> **More Info:** www.akaeaf.org/scholarships.htm

Alpha Kappa Alpha Sorority

Many of the 700 local chapters offer scholarships to qualified high school and college students. Awards are almost exclusively for black women.

> **Award:** Varies
> **Contact:** 773-684-1282
> **More Info:** Alpha Kappa Alpha Sorority, Inc., 5211 S. Greenwood Avenue, Chicago, IL 60615

Alpha Phi Alpha Fraternity

The fraternity provides scholarships to high school students involved in various educational and community projects.

> **Award:** Varies
> **Contact:** 773-373-1819
> **More Info:** Alpha Phi Alpha Fraternity, Inc., 4432 S. Martin Luther King Drive, Chicago, IL 60653

Delta Sigma Theta, Inc.

For the Myra Davis Hemmings Scholarship, applicants must be active, dues-paying members of Delta Sigma Theta and majoring in the performing or creative arts. Applicants must submit transcripts of all college and records. Deadline: March

> **Award:** Varies
> **Deadline:** March
> **Contact:** 202-483-5460 / 202-966-2513
> **More Info:** Delta Sigma Theta, Inc., 1707 New Hampshire Avenue, NW, Washington, DC 20009

IOTA Phi Lambda Business Sorority

Scholarships are offered to minority female undergraduates interested in business careers.

> **Award:** Varies
> **Contact:** Iota Phi Lambda Business Sorority, 811 E. 116th Street, Los Angeles, CA 90059

IOTA Phi Lambda Scholarship Program

Scholarships are offered to black women to increase interest in business careers.

> **Award:** Varies
> **Contact:** Iota Phi Lambda Scholarship Program, 1062 W. Pearl, Jackson MS 39203

OMEGA Wives Scholarship

Applicants must be black females who are William Penn High seniors and who have maintained an 80 percent average in grades 10-12. A transcript must accompany application. Applicants must have participated in school and/or community related activities and is accepted by an accredited school of higher learning.

> **Award:** Varies
> **Contact:** Your high school guidance counselor for further information and an application form.
> **More Info:** William Penn High School, Broad and Master Streets, Philadelphia, PA 19122

Phi Beta Sigma Fraternity

Scholarships, employment referrals, and other programs are available to college-bound black high school students

> **Awards:** Varies
> **Contact:** 202-726-5434
> **More Info:** http://admissions.boisestate.edu/afrischlr.shtml

Phi Delta Kappa International

Students must show interest in pursuing a career within the field of education. Students will be asked to submit an application and have a 3.0 or above GPA.

>Award: $1,500
>Deadline: January 15
>Contact: 800-766-1156
>More Info: Phi Delta Kappa International, 408 Union St., P.O. Box 789, Bloomington, IA 47402

SIGMA GAMMA RHO Sorority National Education Fund, Inc.

The scholarship is available to students with a sincere interest in achieving a higher education. Applicants must be enrolled in or qualified for admission to an institution for higher education and must demonstrate need and scholastic ability.

>Deadline: April 30
>Contact: 6505 Auburnhill Drive, Austin, Texas 78723-705
>More Info: www.sgrho1922.org/nef/nefinfo.pdf

Zeta Delta Phi Sorority

This sorority promotes academic excellence and offers scholarships to qualified black high school students.

>Award: Varies
>Contact: Zeta Delta Phi Sorority, Inc., P.O. Box 157, Bronx, NY 10469

Sports Scholarships

AAU Youth Excel Program Scholarship, Amateur Athletic Union (AAU)

This scholarship is for high school seniors, athletes who maintain a 2.5 minimum GPA. Participate in at least one sanctioned high school sport and show involvement in the community. Must submit an essay on goals accomplished and obstacles. Persevering through adversity is the key ingredient in the awarding of these scholarships.

>Award: $500 - $3,500
>Deadline: Contact for details
>Contact: Amateur Athletic Union, Youth Excel Program Coordinator, P.O. Box 22409, Lake Buena Vista, FL 32830
>More Info: www.aausports.org

Dorothy Harris Endowed Scholarship

This scholarship was established in honor of Dr. Dorothy Harris, pioneer and advocate for women in sports. Its goal is to assist women graduate students pursuing one of the following fields of study: Physical Education, Sport Management, Sport Psychology or Sport Sociology. Any female, American citizen or legal resident graduate student who will be pursuing a full-time course of study at an accredited postgraduate institution is eligible to apply for the scholarship.

> Award: $1,500
> Deadline: December 29
> Contact: 800-227-3988
> More Info: www.womenssportsfoundation.org/cgi-bin/iowa/funding

Ethnic Minority and Women's Enhancement Postgraduate Scholarship for Careers in Athletics

The NCAA awards 13 scholarships to ethnic minorities and 13 scholarships to female college graduates who will be entering their initial year of postgraduate studies. Three additional scholarships are awarded to students who have completed undergraduate study at a Division III institution for both scholarships. The applicant must be seeking admission or have been accepted into a sports administration program that will help him or her obtain a job in intercollegiate athletics.

> Award: $6,000
> Deadline: December 7
> Contact: 317-917-6222
> More Info: www1.ncaa.org/membership/ed_outreach/prof_development/ minority-womens_scholarships.html

Jackie Robinson Foundation Scholarship Fund

Minority students who are high school seniors, have demonstrated high academic achievements, financial need, and leadership potential, and have been accepted to an accredited four-year institution.

> Award: up to $7,200
> Deadline: March 31
> Contact: 212-290-8600
> More Info: www.jackierobinson.org/apply/index.php

National Minority Junior Golf Scholarship Association

Eligible applicants are minority high school seniors who are interested in attending college. Applicants are asked to write a 500-word essay on this question: "One of the principal goals of education and golf is fostering ways for people to respect and get along with individuals who think, dress, look and act differently. How might you make this goal a reality?" Selection is based on academic record, personal recommendations, participation in golf, school and community activities (including employment, extracurricular activities, and other responsibilities), and financial need.

Award: $1,000 (minimum)
Deadline: April 15
Contact: 602-943-8399
More Info: 7226 North 16th Street, Suite 210, Phoenix, AZ 85020

SAMMY Award

This award is open to graduating high school senior scholar athletes, must demonstrate excellence in academics, athletic performance, leadership and community service to be eligible.

Award: $7,500
Deadline: November
Contact: www.whymilk.com

USBC Bowling Scholarships For Young Bowlers

Young bowlers who participate in YABA/USBC leagues/tournaments may be eligible for several national bowling-related scholarship competitions. Adults who are active in providing youth programs may be eligible for national recognition awards. More than $6 million in scholarship money is offered each season by bowling associations and councils, sanctioned tournaments and proprietors throughout the United States.

Award: $1,500
Deadline: November 1
Contact: 800-514-Bowl
More Info: www.bowl.com/scholarships/main.aspx

Women's Sports Foundation

This award is for female high school seniors who demonstrate leadership and athletic ability, and who will be pursuing a full-time course of study at an accredited two or four-year college.

Award: Contact for details
Deadline: December
Contact: 800-227-3988
More Info: www.lifetimetv.com/WoSport

Part Three
Essays/Contests/ Competitions

Some foundations may require you to write an essay or a statement of your plan of study. This can be anywhere from 300 to 1000 words and may include topics as diverse as your career goals, your definition of leadership, or your reasons for wanting to study abroad. This section includes suggestions on how to write a winning essay as well as listings of top funding resources for competitive African American students.

How To Write A Winning Scholarship Essay

Third Person: Be sure to write your essay in third person. This means not using words such as "I", "we" or even "you". Rather, you want to write your essay as if it is a newspaper article or a press release. For instance, suppose the essay question is "What do you think about abortions?" Don't start off saying "I think abortions are…" or "I believe that abortions can…" Instead, just say "Abortions are…" or "Abortions can…"

Organization:	Be sure to organize your essay. This means that you will need a definite introduction, a body, and a conclusion. Be sure to use paragraphs and organize your thoughts. Don't have random thoughts within the essay that don't exactly fit with the flow of the paragraphs.
References:	Use references in your essay to show that you did your research. You can cite a book, a magazine, or even a web site. Whenever you make a claim in your essay that wouldn't be obvious to most people, you should definitely cite where you obtained such a statement. You can also include a few quotes from notable people, but make sure that it appropriately relates to the topic of your essay.
Pay Attention:	Pay attention to the rules. Many people lose essay contests because they don't follow simple rules. For example, if a scholarship contest requires that you put only your name and phone number at the top of your essay—then do just that. Don't decide to add your address and fax number. If they say to email your essay in, don't submit it via postal mail. This may very well be a test to see if you can follow instructions.
No Typos:	Be sure that you spell all words correctly in your essay. Make sure that you use quotation marks, commas, colons, semi-colons, and periods appropriately. Avoid incomplete sentences and run-on sentences.
Make the Deadline:	Shockingly, many applicants try to submit essays after the deadline. Make sure that you get yours in on time. Don't procrastinate. Start early, and submit early.

Think Big…and Small: Don't just apply for the high-end scholarships for $5,000 and up. Keep in mind that these generally are more competitive due to more applicants. Be sure to also apply for the smaller ones, like the $500 and $1,000 scholarships. These opportunities are easier to win because most applicants don't take them very seriously. They also usually have fewer applicants.

Top Funding Resources for Competitive African American Students

A. Patrick Charnon Scholarship

This scholarship is open to current full-time undergraduate students and those who have been accepted to a four-year college or university. Students who value tolerance, compassion and respect for all people in their communities, and who have demonstrated their commitment to theses values by their actions, will be considered for this award. In addition to an official transcript and three letters of recommendation, applicants must submit a typed 2-4 page essay on how community service experiences have shaped their lives; and how they will use their college education to build communities in a manner consistent with Pat Charnon's values of compassion, tolerance, generosity and respect.

Award: $1,500
Deadline: March 31st
Email Only: scholarship@cesresources.org
More Info: www.cesresources.org/charnon.html

AFSCME Family Scholarship

An ongoing program of scholarships is available to children and financially dependent grandchildren of AFSCME members. Under the program, 10 scholarships are awarded annually to selected applicants who meet eligibility requirements. The Scholarship Selection Committee will thoroughly examine all the application materials submitted by each scholarship applicant. In addition to the Official Application Form and the applicant's essay, high school transcript and SAT or ACT results, the selection committee will carefully consider any recommendations or other evidence (e.g., high school activities or academic honors) of the applicant's character or abilities.

Award: $2,000
Deadline: December 31
Contact: 202-429-1000
More Info: www.afscme.org/members/880.cfm

Amber Communications Group (ACGI) Essay Competition

This competition is open to African American high school seniors with at least a 3.0 GPA. Must plan to attend college and pursue a career in the book publishing industry. Applicants must submit an essay (approximately 500 words) about why they want to pursue a career in book publishing along with a letter of recommendation from an English teacher. Mail submissions to Amber Communications Group Essay Competition, 1334 East Chandler Boulevard, Suite 5-D67, Phoenix, AZ 85048 or email to: amberbks@aol.com. Winner must be available to attend the Book Expo America (BEA) where he or she will intern with ACGI during the course of the 3-day event.

    Contact: 602-743-7426
    More Info: www.amberbooks.com
    Deadline: April 15
    Amount: $250 plus travel expenses to BEA

Applegate/Jackson/Parks Future Teacher Scholarship

One scholarship is awarded annually to the education student who best exemplifies the dedication to principle and high professional standards of Carol Applegate, Kay Jackson, and Dr. Anne Parks. Applicants are limited to graduate or undergraduate students majoring in education in institutions of higher learning throughout the United States. Officers, directors and employees of the National Institute for Labor Relations Research, the National Right to Work Committee, Members of the Selection Review Committee and their families are not eligible.

    Award: $1,000
    Deadline: December 31
    Contact: 703-321-9606
    More Info: www.nilrr.org/teachers.htm

Association for Women in Sports Media Scholarship

This scholarship is for undergraduate or graduate women who are seeking careers in sports writing and sports editing. Submit essay, resume, 1 recommendation and 5 clips.

    Award: $1,000
    Deadline: November 1
    Contact: 847-832-7256
    More Info: 325 Waukegan Road, Northfield, IL 60093-2750

Atlas Shrugged Essay Contest

Applicants must write a 1,000-word essay on one of three topics. Essays will be judged on both style and content. Judges will look for writing that is clear, articulate and logically organized. Winning essays must demonstrate an outstanding grasp of the philosophic meaning of Atlas Shrugged. Entrant must be enrolled in a college degree program at the time of entry.

    Award: $50 to $5,000
    Deadline: September 15
    Contact: 949-222-6550
    More Info: www.aynrand.org/site/PageServer?pagename=education_contests_atlas

AWorldConnected Essay Contest

The AWorldConnected Essay Contest is available to full-time undergraduate and graduate students who are 25 years of age or younger. You must watch/read the works indicated on the sponsor's site and write an essay of less than 2,500 words. You may touch on any of the themes raised in the video or article and address any other examples, relevant issues, or ideas that you think the author has neglected.

    Award: $250 to $5000
    Deadline: December 15
    Email Only: jschrock@gmu.edu
    More Info: www.aworldconnected.org/About/pageID.768/default.asp

College Prowler Essay Scholarship - Wachovia Monthly Scholarship

College Prowler and Wachovia are prowling around for the best college application essays in the nation. Have you written an essay for any of your college applications? If so, submit it to the College Prowler - Wachovia Monthly Scholarship.

    Award: $1,000/Month
    Deadline: Last Day of Each Month
    Contact: 800-290-2682
    More Info: www.collegeprowler.com/the_scholarship.asp

Datatel Scholars Foundation Scholarship

Undergraduate and graduate students planning to attend or are currently attending a Datatel Client college or university, or who work at a Datatel non-education Client site and will attend any college or university during the upcoming academic year. You must write an essay that summarizes your educational goals and objectives, and indicate the difference a Datatel Scholars foundation Scholarship would make in your life and to those around you.

> **Award:** $700 - $7,000
> **Deadline:** February
> **Contact:** 800-486-4332
> **More Info:** Datatel Scholars Foundation, 4375 Fair Lakes court, Fairfax, VA 22033

Discovery Channel Young Scientist Challenge

Every year, more than 60,000 children from around the country enter science projects in one of the science and engineering fairs affiliated with Science Service. Six thousand middle school entrants are then nominated by their fair directors to enter their projects in the Discovery Channel Young Scientist Challenge—the only competition of its kind for students in grades 5 through 8. Between June (the deadline for entering) and early September, our judges choose 400 semifinalists among the entries. Students are judged on the scientific merit of their work and, just as importantly, on their ability to communicate the science of their project.

> **Award:** $500 to $20,000
> **Deadline:** June
> **Email Only:** dcysc_science@discovery.com
> **More Info:**
> http://school.discovery.com/sciencefaircentral/dysc/accept/accept.html

Elks National Foundation Most Valuable Student Contest

This contest is for graduating high school seniors who are U.S. citizens with a minimum 3.0 GPA. Applicants do not need to be members or children of members. Application must be submitted to a local chapter.

> **Award:** $1,000 - $15,000
> **Deadline:** Mid-January
> **Contact:** 773-755-4700
> **More Info:** www.elks.org/enf/default.cfm

Ellen Masin Persina Scholarship

This scholarship is open to minority high school seniors who have been accepted to college and plan a career in journalism. Applicants must demonstrate an ongoing interest in journalism through work in high school and/or other media, submit a one-page essay on why they want to pursue a career in journalism and have at least a 2.75 GPA in high school.

    Award: $5,000
    Deadline: March 1
    Contact: 202-662-7500
    More Info: www.press.org

Ellie Wiesel Prize in Ethics Essay Contest

This scholarship is open to full-time juniors and seniors in a college or university. Check the web site for the annual essay questions.

    Award: $500 - $5,000
    Deadline: December
    Contact: 212-490-7777
    More Info: www.eliewieselfoundation.org

FBI Common Knowledge Challenge Scholarship Competition

This competition is available to current students attending a community college, college or university, or graduate school. The intent of the scholarship is to assist the student in understanding what it means to work for the FBI as an agency and as a career path. Students who register for the scholarship competition will be e-mailed a list of FBI web site links from which questions will be derived. The student will answer the questions and receive a score. At the end of each round, the highest scoring student will be awarded a scholarship.

    Awards: $250
    Contact: 954-262-8935
    More Info: www.cksf.org

Fountainhead Essay Contest

Applicant must be a junior or senior in high school. Please see the web site for essay question.

    Award: $50 - $10,000
    Deadline: April 15
    Contact: 949-222-6550
    More Info: www.aynrand.org

Hispanic College Fund Scholarships

The Hispanic College Fund awards scholarships based on both merit and financial need. HCF administers multiple scholarship programs including the Sallie Mae Fund's First in My Family Scholarship Program and the ALPFA Scholarship Program. The minimum eligibility criteria for HCF scholarship programs are: Must be a U.S. citizen or permanent resident residing in the United States; Must be studying full-time in the United States or Puerto Rico; Must have a minimum GPA of a 3.0. To apply for HCF Scholarships you will be required to complete an online application which includes at least one essay, letter of recommendation and resume.

Award: up to $10,000
Deadline: March 15
More Info: http://scholarships.hispanicfund.org

HIV/AIDS Story Writing Contest

This contest involves writing a story about personal vulnerability to HIV/AIDS. Your story can be either fiction or non-fiction. The characters in the story must be impacted by HIV/AIDS. This scholarship contest seeks to inspire 14-22 year olds to examine their personal vulnerability to HIV/AIDS; motivate young people to express themselves in writing so they can share their thoughts and experiences; and to promote positive health behaviors through media written by and for young people.

Award: $2,500
Deadline: December 1
Email Only: contest@selectmedia.org
More Info: www.hearmeproject.org

Holocaust Remembrance Scholarships
2007 Theme / Writing Prompt

Students responding to this year's writing contest should study the Holocaust and then, in an essay of no more than 1,200 words: (a) analyze why it is so vital that the remembrance, history and lessons of the Holocaust be passed to a new generation; and (b) suggest what they, as students, can do to combat and prevent prejudice, discrimination and violence in our world today.

This contest is open to all students age 19 and under who meet the following criteria: (1) are currently enrolled as a high school student in grades 9-12 (including home schooled students) or who are high school seniors who may graduate high school at any time in 2007, or are students who are enrolled in a high school equivalency program; AND (2) are *residents* of either the United States or Mexico or who are United States Citizens living abroad.

> **Award:** $2,500 to $10,000 (plus an all-expense-paid trip to Washington, D.C.)
> **Deadline:** April 30
> **Contact:** 1-866-452-2737
> **More Info:** http://holocaust.hklaw.com/2007/index.asp

Lonzie L. Jones, Jr., Scholarship

All high school seniors must write an essay. Check with local NASCO on annual contest theme.

> **Award:** $1,000 to $2,500
> **Deadline:** April 16
> **Contact:** Lonzie L. Jones, Jr., Scholarship, Sickle Cell Disease Inc., 3345 Wiltshire Blvd, Los Angeles, CA 90010

Maryland Artists Equity Foundation Annual Scholarship Competition

Senior high school students from all Maryland public and private schools, who have applied for entry to an accredited college or university for advanced art studies in the visual arts, are eligible to apply for MAEF scholarships. MAEF looks forward to your entry. Good luck.

> **Award:** $500 up to $3,000 (credited to students' tuition accounts at accredited institutions)
> **Deadline:** February 9
> **Contact:** 410-813-4006
> **More Info:** www.maef.org/

Mensa Education and Research Foundation Scholarship
This scholarship is open to all students (must write a 550-word essay).
> **Award:** Varies
> **Deadline:** Mid-January
> **More Info:** www.merf.us.mensa.org

Michael J. Berkeley Foundation Golf Scholarship
This scholarship assists deserving minority youth in reaching their highest potential in the sport of golf through education, business ventures, or in a professional golf career. The foundation awards scholarships to full-time college students of color who personify Michael J. Berkeley's legacy. The scholarships are awarded on the basis of academic achievement, extracurricular/community involvement, leadership/team skills, financial need, commendations, honors, written communication skills, essays, letters of recommendations and verbal communication skills pursuant to a telephonic interview.
> **Award:** $3,000
> **Contact:** 914-244-1668
> **More Info:** www.mikebfoundation.org/scholarships.html

National Black Nurses Association
The March of Dimes Birth Defect Award is given to black nursing students, with the best essay addressing the "Prevention of Teenage Pregnancy and Decrease in Infant Mortality Rates. Entrants must be members of the National Black Nurses Association and must be enrolled in an LPN/LVN program. Essays will be judged on clarity, innovation of the approach, grammar, style, and format (fewer than 2,500 words).
> **Award:** $1,000
> **Deadline:** May
> **Contact:** 617-266-9703
> **More info:** www.nbna.org/

National Fellowship of Black College Leaders Scholarship

This scholarship was established by former student leaders of Historically Black Colleges and Universities as a way to honor and build upon the legacy of these prestigious and invaluable institutions. Each fall semester, the National Fellowship of Black College Leaders will award a scholarship to an outstanding and deserving student who enrolls or is currently enrolled at an accredited Historically Black College or University. The award will be based on scholastic achievement, financial need, leadership ability, school and community activities, essay and recommendation.

> **Award:** $1,000
> **Deadline:** May 31
> **Email Only:** NFBCL.2006@gmail.com
> **More Info:** www.hbcuconnect.com/NFBCL_Scholarship_Application1.pdf

National Peace Essay Contest

This contest is for students who are in grades 9-12 and are attending public, private or parochial school or participating in a high school correspondence program in any of the fifty states, the District of Columbia, or U.S. Territories.

> **Award:** $1,000
> **Deadline:** February 1
> **Contact:** Institute of Peace
> **More Info:** 1200 17th Street NW, Suite 200, Washington, DC 20036-3011

Nelly's P.I.M.P (Positive. Intellectual. Motivated. Person) Scholarship Contest

The scholarship will be extended to students from all disciplines with no grade restrictions to compete to produce the most unique Pimp Juice or PJ Tight video commercial that best captures the essence of the energized, successful hip hop lifestyle promoted by Nelly's energy drinks. In addition, the contest committee will also consider the student's grade point average, extracurricular activities, and any other relevant factors.

> **Awards:** $500 to $5,000
> **Deadline:** March 3
> **Email Only:** wooty@derrtyent.com
> **More Info:** www.letitloose.com

Siemens Westinghouse Scholarship Competition in Math, Science and Technology

This competition recognizes remarkable talent early on; fostering individual growth for high school students who are willing to challenge themselves through science research. Through this competition, students have an opportunity to achieve national recognition for science research projects that they complete in high school. It is administered by The College Board and funded by the Siemens Foundation. Students may submit research reports either individually or in teams of two or three members. Impartial panels of research scientists from leading universities and national laboratories judge the reports in the initial blind reading.

Award: $1,000 to $6,000
Deadline: October 2
Contact: 877-822-5233
More Info: www.siemens-foundation.org/competition

Society of Plastics Engineers "Wonder of Plastics" International Essay Contest

Open to all junior high and high school students who have demonstrated or expressed an interest in the plastics industry. They must be majoring in or taking courses that would be beneficial to a career in the plastics industry. This would include, but is not limited to, plastics engineering, polymer science, chemistry, physics, chemical engineering, mechanical engineering, and industrial engineering.

Award: $1,000 and $1,000 for school
Deadline: Decided by the individual SPE Sections
Contact: 203-775-0471
More Info: www.4spe.org/awards/essaycontest.php

Signet Classic Student Scholarship Essay Contest

Each English teacher may only submit 1 junior and 1 senior essay. Entrants must be a full time 11th, or 12th grade student between the ages of 16-18. Essay should be at least 2 but not more than 3 double spaced pages. All sole work of the entrant. All entries will become the property of Signet Classic (Penguin Putnam, Inc.) and will not be returned.

Award: $1,000 (5 scholarships awarded annually)
Deadline: Contact for details
Contact: Penguin Putnam Inc.
More Info: 375 Hudson St., New York, NY 10014

Summer Mamashealth.com Scholarship Award

Available to freshman, sophomore, junior and senior students attending a college or university in the United States or Canada. Applicants must submit an essay, maximum of 750 words, which addresses the following question: "Should illegal immigrants be eligible to receive free health-care." Applicants must submit college transcripts to be eligible for this award.

> **Award:** $600
> **Deadline:** August 31
> **More Info:** www.mamashealth.com/aboutus/scholarship3.asp

Swackhamer Peace Essay Contest

Applicant must submit an essay and fulfill the requirements of the Nuclear Age Peace Foundation.

> **Award:** $500 - $1,000
> **Deadline:** June
> **Contact:** 805-965-3443
> **More Info:** www.wagingpeace.org

TechStudents.net Scholarship

The TechStudents.net Scholarship is available to vocational/technical, community college, four-year college and graduate students who are pursuing degrees in technology-related fields including, but not limited to: computer science, information technology, graphic and web design and information systems. Selection for this award will be based on creativity, content and usability of your application. A brief essay outlining technology advice for entrepreneurs and small businesses is also required.

> **Award:** $500
> **Deadline:** January 13
> **Email Only:** info@techstudents.net
> **More Info:** www.techstudents.net/TechScholarship.asp

The Charles Shafae' Scholarship Fund

This fund awards two scholarships each year to winners of the Paper-check Essay Contest. You must write a minimum 1,000 word essay on five suggested topics. There is no maximum word count. All five topics must be covered in your essay. We will focus on grammar and the clear presentation of ideas. Include a Works Cited page with a minimum of three sources. The essay must follow the Modern Language Association (MLA) system for documenting sources, which is set forth in the MLA Handbook for Writers of Research Papers, 6th edition.

> **Award:** $500
> **Deadline:** June 1
> **Contact:** 866-693-3348
> **More Info:** www.papercheck.com/scholarship.asp

The Collegiate Inventors Competition

This competition is open to students who have been enrolled full time in a college or university over the past 12 months. You must submit an original idea, process or technology that will be judged on originality and inventiveness, as well as on its potential value to society (socially, environmentally, and economically), and on its range or scope of use. Up to four students may work together as a team. However, only one prize will be awarded per entry.

> **Award:** $3,000 to $10,000
> **Deadline:** June 1
> **Contact:** 330-849-6887
> **More Info:** www.invent.org/collegiate/overview.html

The "Dream Deferred" Essay Contest on Civil Rights

This essay contest takes its title from a 1951 poem by Langston Hughes: "What Happens to a Dream Deferred?" The poem helped propel the civil rights movement in the United States. Today, it will hopefully inspire you to describe your dream deferred for the Middle East, which the United Nations calls the world's least free region. The contest has two parts: one for Middle Eastern youth (25 and younger) and one for American youth (25 and younger). To participate, write a brief essay (600-2,000 words) addressing one of three questions.

> **Award:** $500 to 2,000
> **Deadline:** January 30
> **More Info:** www.hamsaweb.org/essay-contest.php

The Dr. Robert Rufflo Scholarship Fund

Are you a science wiz with good writing ability? The Robert Rufflo Scholarship Fund awards two scholarships per year to high school and college students enrolled in accredited schools in the U.S. Scholarships are granted for exemplary work in a variety of applied and basic science fields. Work may focus on original research, a research review, or critical essay. The scholarship will be awarded for what is judged to be the best research paper, research review or critical essay in the sciences. The emphasis of evaluation is on quality background research and effective communication in writing.

> **Award:** $500
> **Deadline:** June
> **Contact:** 608-577-0642
> **More Info:** www.metavue.com/Scholarships/mvcp_Scholarship.asp?id=4

The Olive W. Garvey Fellowship

This fellowship is available to undergraduate and graduate students under the age of 35. Since 1974, the internationally acclaimed Olive W. Garvey Fellowship program has awarded fellowships biennially to outstanding college students around the world through a competitive essay contest. Your essay must be 3,000 words or less and address a designated topic.

> **Award:** $1,000 to $10,000
> **Deadline:** May 1
> **Contact:** 510-632-1366
> **More Info:** www.independent.org/garvey.html

The Royce Osborn Minority Student Scholarship

The ASRT Education and Research Foundation Royce Osborn Minority Student Scholarship program provides scholarships for academically out-standing, minority students attending an entry-level radiological sciences program. The essay contest offers you an opportunity to help us become acquainted with you in a different way than grades, test scores and other objective data. It allows you to show your ability to organize your thoughts and to express yourself.

> **Award:** $4,000
> **Deadline:** February 1
> **Contact:** 800-444-2778, Ext. 2541
> **More Info:** www.asrt.org

The Writer's Digest Annual Short Short Story Competition

Writer's Digest is now accepting entries in the Annual Short Short Story Competition. We are looking for fiction that's bold, brilliant...but brief. Send us your best in 1,500 words or fewer. All entries must be in English, original, unpublished, and not submitted elsewhere until the winners are announced. Writer's Digest reserves the right to publish the First-Place story. The 1st through 25th-place manuscripts will be printed in a special competition collection, published by Trafford Publishing.

Award: $50 to $3,000
Deadline: December
Contact: 888-232-4444 ext 1587
More Info: www.writersdigest.com/contests/shortshort

Thomson Course Help Desk Scholarship Contest

Contest is open to U.S. citizens who are enrolled in a U.S. public or private college or university or career school and are enrolled in a Help Desk course at the time of entry. One scholarship winner will be chosen to win tuition reimbursement dollars. The winner will be selected on the basis of the thoughtfulness of the essay. Decisions by the judges are final and binding. The winner will be posted at the course.com/helpdesk web site. Odds of winning depend upon the number of entries received.

Award: $1,000
Deadline: May 12
Contact: 203-775-0471
More Info: www.course.com/helpdesk/rules.cfm

Video Contest for College Students

The annual contest is open to all students currently enrolled in undergraduate or graduate programs at colleges or universities. Films must be five minutes or less in length and may be submitted as a standard, full-sized NTSC-format VHS tape or as Region 1 or regionless DVDs. Entries will be judged on overall impact, effectiveness in conveying theme, artistic merit and technical proficiency. Videos become the property of The Christophers and will not be returned.

Award: $3,000
Deadline: June 8
Contact: 212-759-4050
More Info: www.christophers.org/contests.html

Voice of Democracy Scholarship Program, Veterans of Foreign Wars

This competition is for U.S. high school students in grades 9 –12. Students must submit a 3-5 minute essay for local competition. Selected candidates compete on state and national levels. Contact your high school counselor or local VFW Post.

> **Award:** Up to $25,000
> **Deadline:** November 15
> **Contact:** 816-756-3390
> **More Info:** www.chci.org

Washington Urban League Grand Met/National Urban League Essay Contest

Participants must be entering college freshmen or undergraduate college students who will be attending an accredited institution of higher learning. Awards will be made payable to the institution. Essays must be between 500 and 1,000 words and be typewritten and double spaced or legibly handwritten and must include participant's full name and permanent address. Entries will be judged for content, originality, organization, style, grammar, spelling, punctuation, and neatness.

> **Award:** $1,000
> **Contact:** High school guidance counselor/College counselor for additional information and this year's topic and deadline.
> **More Info:** Deputy Director, Northern Virginia Branch, Washington Urban League, Inc., 901 N. Washington St., #202, Alexandria, VA 22314

Writer's Digest Poetry Competition

We're pleased to announce the only Writer's Digest competition exclusively for poets! Regardless of style—rhyming, free verse, haiku and more—if your poems are 32 lines or fewer, we want them all. The entry fee is $10 for your first poem and $5 for each additional poem. You may enter as many poems as you wish. All entries must be in English, original, unpublished, and not submitted elsewhere until the winners are announced. Writer's Digest reserves the one-time publication rights to the 1st through 25th-place winning entries to be published in a Writer's Digest publication.

> **Contact:** Refer to the web site below for details.
> **More Info:** www.writersdigest.com/contests/poetry/index.asp

Part Four

The Financial Aid Process

At the outset of the scholarship seeking process, be sure to articulate your plan of study in order to increase your chances of getting funding. Ask yourself the following questions....the answers will help to clarify your own needs, which can then help you determine the kind of funding for which you might quality:

- What will be my major area of study or research?
- Will I be studying part-time or full-time, or am I just planning to take individual classes?
- Where do I plan to study?
- When do I plan to enroll?
- How does my plan of study fit into my overall personal and Career Goals?

Budgeting for College

Once you have confirmed your goals, figure out the costs for your studies. Your annual budget for your education will include tuition, room and board, books, travel and other living expenses. Consider whether you will be a "resident" student attending a state university and living on campus or an out-of-state/district student. If you are studying out of state, you will likely pay a surcharge, and tuition at private institutions will be significantly higher.

Now that you have a good idea of where you plan to study and how much it will cost, your first stop should be the financial aid office at that particular college or university. Counselors there will be able to provide you with information on sources of funding—both federal and state government loans/grants, as well as private sources. Armed with this guide and the information from the financial aid office, your chances of financing your college education have increased significantly.

Keep in mind that while many scholarships are based on merit and/or performance, foundations typically base their awards on need and will ask what options you have exhausted before you submit an application to them. Therefore, you should have a firm idea of what support, if any, you can expect to receive from the government or from the college itself before you submit your application. Among other things, foundations will want to know about your:

- Personal Savings
- Family Contributions
- School-based Scholarships/Fellowships
- Governmental Grants/Loans
- Work-Study Assistance

Applying For Funds

Armed with a list of funders that closely match your funding needs, you are now ready to send in your applications. When you read the guidelines of the funders you identified as "prospectives", you will quickly realize that there is no standard application form.

Each foundation has its own unique funding guidelines and application procedures, and many colleges that award scholarships have their own application forms as well.

Successful Application Checklist

There are certain strategies you can adopt to strengthen your application.

❑ A first step would be to fill out the Free Application for Federal Student Aid (FAFSA) to determine how much your family is able to contribute toward your college education. All financial aid packages expect you to pay something toward your education. Experts also encourage you to go to your local public library and diligently research scholarship sources that can be found in the many volumes on scholarships, grants, fellowships, etc.

❑ Start as early as possible in your scholarship seeking process. Pay attention to deadlines noted in the guidelines; each foundation will have its own deadline to apply. It is important for you to do your research well in advance so that you are able to submit your application on time. Sometimes submitting your application well in advance of the deadline will prove advantageous.

❑ Put yourself in the scholarship funder's shoes and think about why she/he might be interested in funding you. Express your unique attributes that are appealing to the funder. Try to be as original as possible.

❑ Make sure your application leaves a strong and positive impression of who you are. Pay attention to vocabularies the funder uses and incorporate them in your application.

❑ Be systematic in following through with all requirements stated in the guidelines. Ensure that your application is complete, and make photocopies of the entire application packet so that you can use the copies as working drafts.

❑ When you fill out the application, make sure it is correct and complete. Errors decrease your chance at a scholarship opportunity. As with the scholarship admissions application, you should take this step toward college seriously. Allocate your time and stay centered. You can do it!

❏ Ask someone who has strong grammar and writing skills to review and comment on your application so that you can revise it before submitting it.

❏ Good record keeping is important as well. If you have already applied for federal or state grants or loans, then you are likely familiar with the paperwork that is required. Depending on the foundation, many of the same documents will be required, including financial statements, tax forms, along with your resume.

❏ If you are granted an interview with the financial aid officer or a prospective funder, be prepared to discuss your background academic achievements, future plans, personal value structure, hobbies and interests.

Here are a series of questions to ask yourself in order to further improve your chances of success:

- Did I complete the application in full?

- Did I submit every document required?

- Did I proofread everything?

- Did I make a copy of the full application for my files?

- Did I call to verify that the application was received?

- Did I ask about the possibility of getting an interview?

If you are fortunate enough to be awarded a scholarship from a foundation, it goes without saying that you need to send a thank you letter. Keep the letter short and simple. You will need to notify the college you are attending of any scholarship funds you receive so that your financial aid can be adjusted accordingly. You'll probably need to reapply each year, since most scholarships are offered on an annual basis.

Choosing Your College or University

Tuition and College Choice

Financial considerations are important when choosing a college or university. However, don't let cost determine what college you are considering. Also, don't wait too long to research financial opportunities—deadlines vary at each and it's important to know what the scholarship/grant covers and for how long.

- Many scholarships and grants are based on financial need.

- In addition, your SAT scores, grade point average, class rank and extracurricular activities may be taken into consideration.

- Low-interest rate loans for tuition. Even though a scholarship is more desirable, the investment in your future is worth it.

- Work study programs. Make sure this program won't distract you from maintaining your good grades. Try to choose one that teaches you skills you can use to market yourself in the future.

Applying To College—Step-By-Step Preparation

- Begin researching colleges in your freshman year of high school.

- Begin applying in your sophomore year of high school; the absolute latest you should apply is the early fall of your senior year.

- Contact colleges that interest you most and have them send you their materials; visit them too if possible (we have provided you all HBCU's web site addresses and phone numbers—do the research!)

- Narrow your search down—if possible—to three colleges or universities that you like most. You may get accepted by all three. By the early part of your senior year, you will be able to make your final decision on which college or university you want to attend. While you wait, you will still have time to apply to other colleges or universities that meet your needs.

- SAT (Scholastic Aptitude Test) and/or ACT (American College Test) are very important to college admission. Make sure you're ready by taking preparation courses prior to the actual test.

- Class rank is important. Completion of certain high school course requirement (i.e. four units of English, three to four units of math—algebra level or higher, two units of science, three units of social studies, and two or three units of a foreign language). Your guidance counselor can help you determine the right course of action.

- Honors and awards complement your ability to win scholarships and gain acceptance. For instance, when applying to a very competitive school (if by chance you don't meet the regular admission requirements: honors, extracurricular activities, recommendations in and out of school) show that you care enough to give more than 100%. Specifically, write about any honors you have not received only at school, but also in your community or at your church. This involvement could include the student council, sports, the honors society, the school newspaper or yearbook, the debate team or community work. If you haven't, start now.

- Get references. Ask up to four people to write a letter for you. Teachers are good candidates for this, as are coaches, employers, church members or community service co-workers. Provide them with a short yet informative biography on you that includes information about your grade point average, courses taken, sports and/or other extracurricular activities, community and church service, and anything else of special note about you.

The Application Process

Filling Out Your Scholarship Application Form

Don't look at this process as one giant project. You can generally expect to receive an application, an essay form and an information booklet. The booklet will give you information about deadlines, instructions for completing the application, requirements, admission criteria, etc., including special requirements, financial aid, and housing availability.

- Allocate a quiet hour or two per day to devote to the process where you focus on nothing but what you need to get done. Do as much as you can each day.

- Sit in a well-lit area with a cool drink. Relax and focus.

- Give yourself deadlines for certain items you need to complete. Make sure you provide all information that is requested; make sure to be clear and concise.

- Important! Ask your guidance counselor or a teacher to review your applications with you before mailing them out.

- Give yourself a pat on the back as you reach and meet each deadline.

The application process will give you good experience in time and project management that will work well for you in both college and in your career!

Ron Brown Scholar Program Application
(This application may be photocopied)
RETURN TO: Ron Brown Scholar Program, 1160 Pepsi Place, Suite 206, Charlottesville, VA 22901

CHECK ONE:

☐ I am submitting my application by November 1st of my senior year in high school in order to be considered for the Ron Brown Scholar Program and to have my application materials forwarded to a select & limited number of additional scholarship providers. I understand that I am still responsible for applying to all scholarship programs for which I am interested.

☐ I am submitting my application by January 9th of my senior year in high school in order to be considered for only the Ron Brown Scholar Program.

Applicants must be U.S. citizens or permanent residents, Black or African American and current high school seniors at the time of their application. College students are not eligible to apply. Application materials must be submitted in one packet. Transcripts and letters of recommendation should not be sent under separate cover. SAT/ACT scores must be included on the application at the time it is mailed. Incomplete, e-mailed or faxed applications will not be considered.

PERSONAL DATA (Type or print in black or blue ink only.)

Social Security Number _____   Are you a U.S. Citizen? ☐ Yes ☐ No

If non-U.S. Citizen, please provide your U.S. Permanent Resident Card Number _____

Full Legal Name _____ Last _____ First _____ Middle _____ Male/Female

Permanent Address _____ Street

City _____ State _____ Zip

Date of Birth _____ Telephone # _____ Cell # _____ E-Mail Address

High School _____ Name _____ Street

City _____ State _____ Zip

List below your scores and dates you have taken or will take the following (you may submit SAT or ACT).

SAT

Date	V/CR	Math	Writing	Date	V/CR	Math	Writing	Date	V/CR	Math	Writing

ACT   AP /IB Tests (optional)

Composite Score/Writing Score/Date	Composite Score/Writing Score/Date	Subject/Score	Subject/Score

SAT Subject Tests (optional)

Writing _____ Score/Date   Math _____ Score/Date   Other _____ Subject/Score/Date

TO BE COMPLETED BY A SCHOOL REPRESENTATIVE

Name _____   Title _____

School _____   State _____ Telephone _____ FAX _____

1. Applicant's Name _____   Cum. GPA _____

2. Class Rank _____   Class Size _____

If rank is not available, please approximate the student's position to the nearest tenth from the top and/or provide a grade distribution for the class _____.

3. Do you weight the grades or exclude certain courses to determine rank and/or GPA? _____
If yes, please provide us with a key to this information if it is not already available on the transcript.

4. Of this candidate's graduating class, approximately _____ percent will attend a four-year college.

5. Please submit an official transcript and school profile with application materials. All application materials must be submitted in one packet.

Ron Brown Scholar Program Application—Page 2

Final Deadline January 9th (postmarked)

APPLICANT: *Please respond to the following questions. Attach your typed responses to this form.*

1. Please list your extracurricular, community, employment or other activities in order of their importance to you. Indicate the dates you participated in the activity, positions held and the number of hours per week you spend on each activity. We realize that the way you spend your time outside the classroom may be affected by factors beyond your control, such as the need to work.

2. List any significant awards or honors you have received during high school for academic or extracurricular achievements.

3. Essays: You must respond to both (A) and (B). Each essay should be no longer than 500 words.

    (A) Choose the one activity you listed as most important in question #1 and tell us why it is significant.

    (B) Submit one essay that you plan to send or have sent as part of a college application. This may be on any topic. If your college application did not require an essay, please submit an essay on the topic of your choice.

4. Please ask two individuals who know you well to submit letters of recommendation. At least one letter should be from a teacher or other school professional.

5. Please submit an official transcript and school profile with application materials.

Application materials must be mailed in one packet. Transcripts and letters of recommendation should not be sent under separate cover. To verify receipt of your application, include a self-addressed stamped envelope. A photograph is optional. Incomplete, e-mailed or faxed applications will not be considered. We suggest that you keep copies of your application materials. Semi-finalists will be contacted in March and winners will be announced on our web site in April. We regret that we are unable to individually notify other applicants of the decision on their applications.

The Ron Brown Scholarships are reserved for Black or African American high school seniors and may be used at accredited four-year institutions. If you have questions, please call, send e-mail or visit our web site.

TO BE COMPLETED BY PARENT OR GUARDIAN

Father/Male Guardian	Mother/Female Guardian
_____	_____
Name	Name
_____	_____
Relationship	Relationship
_____	_____
Occupation	Occupation
_____	_____
Adjusted Gross Income (previous year IRS 1040)	Adjusted Gross Income (previous year IRS 1040)
_____	_____
Estimated Adjusted Gross Income (current year)	Estimated Adjusted Gross Income (current year)
_____	_____
# Exemptions Claimed	# Exemptions Claimed

Parents marital status: ☐ Single ☐ Married ☐ Separated ☐ Divorced ☐ Widowed
If parents are not married, please indicate with whom you reside:_____
Ages of Applicant's Siblings _____ # of Siblings Attending College next year _____

We certify that the information provided is true and complete to the best of our knowledge. We understand that if the applicant has applied under the November 1st deadline, application materials will be forwarded to a select and limited number of additional scholarship providers. Additionally, the applicant is still responsible for applying to all scholarship programs for which they may be interested. Semi-finalists may be asked to provide information about the non-custodial parent or step-parent financial contributions. If required, we agree to provide proof of this information, including copies of income tax returns. We realize that if documentation is not provided, the applicant may be deemed ineligible for this scholarship.

_____   _____
Applicant's Signature/Date   Parent or Guardian's Signature/Date

Web site: www.ronbrown.org   E-mail: franh@ronbrown.org   Telephone: 434 964-1588

Let's Review!!

The Financial Aid Process In Summary:

1. Get a financial aid application from the Financial Aid Office of the college or university in which you are interested. PAY SPECIAL ATTENTION TO THE DEADLINES. Don't wait until you've been accepted as a student.

a. Financial Aid Officers at your chosen university will develop a Financial Aid Package.

b. You'll receive an award letter that outlines their offer.

c. It could take up to 2-3 months to receive such a letter.

d. You can accept all, part or none of the financial aid package that has been offered to you.

    The award letter shows the total cost of attending the college in question, the type and amount of aid you've been awarded, and your family's expected contribution. **Respond to the award letter immediately. This is a must!**

2. Complete the Free Application for Federal Student Aid (FAFSA). Mail in the form as soon as possible after January 3 to be eligible to receive financial aid for the following fall. Keep a copy for your records.

a. After you send in your FASA, you will receive your processed Student Aid Report (SAR) within 4 to 8 weeks The SAR includes your expected family contribution, which is directly tied to the amount of the financial award you will receive. Sign and submit the SAR to the university you have chosen.

Financial awards for fall and spring are paid in two equal payments at the beginning of each semester. The choice is up to you and the type of aid you want.

Part Five

Historically Black Colleges and Universities (HBCUs)

Profiles of Historically Black Colleges and Universities

There are more than 100 four-year Historically Black Colleges and Universities within the continental United States and its territories. For your convenience, we have included an alphabetical listing of each college and university by name. We have also provided you the direct phone number and web site address for each HBCU institution.

Historically Black Colleges and Universities offer quality educations. All of them take a strong interest in your growth and development—both academically and personally. Be sure to pick the best one that meets your financial need and academic endeavors. However, any one of these fine HBCU institutions can fulfill your goals of obtaining a higher education.

When choosing the best college or university for the type of educational experience that you seek, there are several criteria that you consider before you commit.

For example, there are location, size, tuition costs for you to consider. What are the areas of study and the degrees offered? What types of internship programs do they offer? What about Greek letter and community outreach organizations that you may want to participate? Is a sports program important to you? You need to know what your university or college offers for a totally well-rounded experience.

Location:

- Close—visit frequently
- Far from home—independence

Size:

- Larger colleges and universities offer more courses of study and advanced degree programs, plus a more diverse student body and faculty.

- Smaller colleges and universities are more accessible. There's more individualized attention and a family atmosphere

Consider this: HBCUs are a source of accomplishment and great pride for the African American community as well as the entire nation. While personal growth and cultural enrichment are important, completing your degree and good grades must be your utmost goal. Whether you decide to attend an HBCU or not, consider the following criteria when you make your choice:

- Select a college or university based on the areas of study it provides (i.e. pre-med/medical, communications or journalism, business, law, and/or internship programs). Choose one that has the strongest reputation (renown) for your degree choice.

- What is the percentage rate of the successful professionals who have graduated from the college or university in your area of intended study (important for future employers and alumni networks).

- If you haven't made up your mind about a career choice, select a college with a strong liberal arts program. It should have a diverse enough degree program, so you won't be limited in your choices.

- Whatever you decide, talk it over with your parents, guidance counselor or mentor. The ultimate decision is yours.

Contact Information For Historically Black Colleges and Universities

Alabama A&M University
4900 Meridian Street
Huntsville, Alabama 35811
256.372.5000
www.aamu.edu

Alabama State University
915 South Jackson Street
Montgomery, Alabama 36101-0271
(334) 229-4984
www.alasu.edu

Albany State University
504 College Drive
Albany, Georgia 31705
(229) 430-4646
www.asurams.edu

Alcorn State University
1000 ASU Drive #930
Alcorn State, Mississippi 39096
(601) 877-6100
www.alcorn.edu

Allen University
1530 Harden Street
Columbia, South Carolina 29204
(803) 376-5700
www.allenuniversity.edu

Arkansas Baptist College
1600 Bishop Street
Little Rock, Arkansas 72202-6099
(501) 374-7856
www.arbaptcol.edu

Barber-Scotia College
145 Cabarrus Ave. - West
Concord, North Carolina 28025
(704) 789-2900
www.b-sc.edu

Benedict College
1600 Harden Street
Columbia, South Carolina 29204
(803) 253-5143 or (800) 868-6598
www.benedict.edu

Bennett College
900 East Washington Street
Greensboro, North Carolina 27401-3239
800-413-5323
www.bennett.edu

Bethune Cookman College
640 Mary McLeod Bethune Blvd.
Daytona Beach, Florida 32114-3099
(386) 481-2000 or (800) 448-0228
www.bethune.cookman.edu

Bishop State Community College
351 North Broad Street
Mobile, Alabama 36603-5898
(251) 690-6801
www.bscc.cc.al.us

Bluefield State College
219 Rock Street
Bluefield, West Virginia 24701-2198
(304) 327-4000
www.bluefieldstate.edu

Bowie State University
14000 Jericho Park Road
Bowie, Maryland 20715
(301) 860-4000
www.bowiestate.edu

Central State University
1400 Brush Row Road
P.O. Box 1004
Wilberforce, Ohio 45384-3002
(937) 376-6011
www.centralstate.edu

Charles Drew University
1731 East 120th Street
Los Angeles, California 90059
(323) 563-4800
www.cdrewu.edu

Cheyney University of Pennsylvania
Cheyney and Creek Roads
Cheyney, Pennsylvania 19319-0019
(610) 399-2000
www.cheyney.edu

Chicago State University
9501 South King Drive
Chicago, Illinois 60628
(773) 995-2513
www.csu.edu

Claflin University
400 Magnolia Street N.E.
Orangeburg, South Carolina 29115
(803) 535-5000 or (800) 922-1276
www.claflin.edu

Clark Atlanta University
223 James P. Brawley Drive, SW
Atlanta, Georgia 30314
(404) 880-8000 or (800) 688-3228
www.cau.edu

Clinton Junior College
1029 Crawford Road
Rock Hill, South Carolina 29730
(803) 327-7402 or (888) 458-5816
www.clintonjuniorcollege.edu

Coahoma Community College
3240 Friars Point Road
Clarksdale, Mississippi 38614-9799
(662) 627-2571
www.ccc.cc.ms.us

Concordia College
1804 Green Street
Selma, Alabama 36701
(334) 874-5700
www.concordiaselma.edu

Coppin State University
2500 West North Avenue
Baltimore, Maryland 21216
(410) 951-3600
www.coppin.edu

CUNY -The Medgar Evers College
1650 Bedford Avenue
Brooklyn, New York 11225
(718) 270-6024
www.mec.cuny.edu

Delaware State University
1200 North DuPont Highway
Dover, Delaware 19901
(302) 857-6060
www.desu.edu

Denmark Technical College
P.O. Box 327
Denmark, South Carolina 29042
(803) 793-5176
www.denmarktech.com

Dillard University
2601 Gentilly Boulevard
New Orleans, Louisiana 70122-3097
(504)283-8822
www.dillard.edu

Edward Waters College
1658 Kings Road
Jacksonville, Florida 32209
(904) 355-3030 or (888) 898-3191
www.ewc.edu

Elizabeth City State University
1704 Weeksville Road
Elizabeth City, North Carolina 27909
(252) 335-3400 or (800) 347-ECSU
www.ecsu.edu

Fayetteville State University
1200 Murchison Road
Fayetteville, North Carolina 28301-4298
(910) 672-1111
www.uncfsu.edu

Fisk University
1000 17th Avenue North
Nashville, Tennessee 37208
(615)329-8500
www.fisk.edu

Florida A&M University
FHAC, Lee Hall Suite 303
Tallahassee, Florida 32307
(850) 599-3000
www.famu.edu

Florida Memorial College
15800 Northwest 42 Avenue
Miami, Florida 33054
(305) 625-3600
www.fmc.edu

Fort Valley State University
1005 State University Drive
Fort Valley, Georgia 31030
(478)825-6280
www.fvsu.edu

Gadsden State Community College
600 Valley Street
Gadsden, Alabama 35902-0227
(256) 549-8672
www.gadsdenstate.edu/campus.htm

Grambling State University
100 Main Street
Grambling, Louisiana 71245
(318) 274-6118
www.gram.edu

Hampton University
Hampton, Virginia 23668
(757) 727-5000 or (800) 624-3328
www.hamptonu.edu

Harris-Stowe State College
3026 Laclede Avenue
St. Louis, Missouri 63103
(314) 340-3300
www.hssc.edu

Hinds Community College
55 E Main Street
P.O. Box 1100
Raymond, Mississippi 39154-1100
(601) 857-5261 or 1-800-HINDSCC
www.hindscc.edu

Howard University
2400 Sixth Street Northwest
Washington, District of Columbia 20059
(202) 806-6100
www.howard.edu

Huston-Tillotson College
900 Chicon Street
Austin, Texas 78702-2795
(512) 505-3000
www.htu.edu

Interdenominational Theological Center
700 Martin Luther King Jr. Drive, Southwest
Atlanta, Georgia 30314
404-527-7792
www.itc.edu

J.F. Drake State Technical College
3421 Meridian Street, North
Huntsville, Alabama 35811
(256) 539-8161 or (888) 413-7253
www.dstc.cc.al.us/

Jackson State University
1400 JR Lynch Street
Jackson, Mississippi 39217
(800) 848-6817
www.jsums.edu

Jarvis Christian College
P.O. Box 1470
Hawkins, Texas 75765
(903) 769-5700
www.jarvis.edu

Johnson C. Smith University
100 Beatties Ford Road
Charlotte, North Carolina 28216
(704) 378-1000
www.jcsu.edu

Kentucky State University
400 East Main Street
Frankfort, Kentucky 40601
(502)597-6000
www.kysu.edu

Knoxville College
901 College Street NW
Knoxville, Tennessee 37921
(865) 524-6603
www.knoxvillecollege.edu

Lane College
545 Lane Avenue
Jackson, Tennessee 38301
(731) 426-7500
www.lanecollege.edu

Langston University
P.O. Box 907
Langston, Oklahoma 73050
(405) 466-2231
www.lunet.edu

Lawson State Community College
3060 Wilson Road, SW
Birmingham, Alabama 35221
(205) 929-6309
www.ls.cc.al.us

Lemoyne-Owen College
807 Walker Avenue
Memphis, Tennessee 38126
(901) 774-9090 or (800) 737-7778
www.loc.edu

Lewis College of Business
17370 Meyers Road
Detroit, Michigan 48235
(313) 862-6300
www.lewiscollege.edu

Lincoln University -Missouri
820 Chestnut
Jefferson City, Missouri 65102-0029
(573) 681-5000
www.lincolnu.edu

Lincoln University -Pennsylvania
MSC#163, P.O. Box 179
Lincoln University, Pennsylvania 19352
(610) 932-1209 or (800) 790-0191
www.lincoln.edu

Livingstone College
701 West Monroe Street
Salisbury, North Carolina 28144
(704) 216-6001 or (800) 835-3435
www.livingstone.edu

Mary Holmes College
P.O. Drawer 1257
West Point, Mississippi 39773
(662) 495-5100 or (800) 634-2749 MS Only
www.maryholmes.edu

Meharry Medical College
1005 DB Todd Boulevard
Nashville, Tennessee 37208-3599
(615) 327-6111
www.mmc.edu

Miles College
5500 Myron-Massey Boulevard
Fairfield, Alabama 350640937
(205) 929-1000
www.miles.edu

Mississippi Valley State University
14000 Highway 82 West
Itta Bena, Mississippi 38941-1400
(662) 254-3347, (800) 844-6885 (In state)
www.mvsu.edu

Morehouse College
830 Westview Drive Southwest
Atlanta, Georgia 30314
(404) 681-2800 or (800) 851-1254
www.morehouse.edu

Morehouse School of Medicine
720 Westview Drive
Atlanta, Georgia 30310-1495
(404) 752-1500
www.msm.edu

Morgan State University
1700 East Coldspring Lane
Baltimore, Maryland 21251
(443) 885-3185 or (800) 332-6674
www.morgan.edu

Morris Brown College
643 Martin Luther King Jr. Dr
Atlanta, Georgia 30314
(404) 739-1000
www.morrisbrown.edu

Morris College
100 West College Street
Sumter, South Carolina 29150
(803) 934-3200
www.morris.edu

Norfolk State University
700 Park Avenue
Norfolk, Virginia 23504-8026
(757) 238-6000
www.nsu.edu

North Carolina A&T State University
1601 East Market Street
Greensboro, North Carolina 27411
(800) 443-8964
www.ncat.edu

North Carolina Central University
1801 Lawson Street
Durham, North Carolina 27707
(919) 560-6100
www.nccu.edu/index1.shtml

Oakwood College
7000 Adventist Boulevard NW
Huntsville, Alabama 35896
(256) 726-7000 or (800) 824-5312
www.oakwood.edu

Paine College
1235 15th Street
Augusta, Georgia 30901-3182
(706) 821-8200
www.paine.edu

Paul Quinn College
3837 Simpson Stuart Road
Dallas, Texas 75241
(214) 376-1000 or (800) 237-2648
www.pqc.edu

Philander Smith College
One Trudie Kibbe Reed Dr
Little Rock, Arkansas 72202
(501) 375-9845
www.philander.edu

Prairie View A&M University
P.O. Box 2777
Prairie View, Texas 77446-3089
(936) 857-3311
www.pvamu.edu

Rust College
150 Rust Avenue
Holly Springs, Mississippi 38635-2328
(662) 252-8000 or (888) 886-8469, x4059
www.rustcollege.edu

Saint Augustine's College
1315 Oakwood Ave.
Raleigh, North Carolina 27610
(919) 516-4000
www.st-aug.edu

Saint Paul's College
115 College Drive
Lawrenceville, Virginia 23868
(434) 848-6431 or (800) 678-7071
www.saintpauls.edu

Savannah State University
P.O. Box 20449
Savannah, Georgia 2,594
(912) 356-2181 or (800) 788-0478
www.savstate.edu

Selma University
1501 Lapsley Street
Selma, Alabama 36701
(334) 872-2533 x18
www.stateuniversity.com/universities/AL/Selma_University.html

Shaw University
118 East South Street
Raleigh, North Carolina 27601
(919) 546-8650
www.shawuniversity.edu

Shelton State Community College
9500 Old Greensboro Road
Tuscaloosa, Alabama 35405
(205) 391-2214
www.shelton.cc.al.us

Shorter College
604 Locust Street
North Little Rock, Arkansas 72114
(501) 374-6305
www.shortercollege.4t.com

South Carolina State University
300 College Street NE
Orangeburg, South Carolina 29117
(803) 536-7000
www.scsu.edu

Southern University and A&M College
Harding Blvd.
Baton Rouge, Louisiana 70813
(225) 771-4500
www.subr.edu

Southwestern Christian College
P.O. Box 10
Terrel, Texas 75160
(972) 524-3341 or (800) 925-9357
www.swcc.edu

Spelman College
350 Spelman Lane Southwest
Atlanta, Georgia 30314
(404) 681-3643
www.spelman.edu

St. Philips College
1801 Martin Luther King Drive
San Antonio, Texas 78203
(210) 531-3200
www.accd.edu/spc/spcmain/spc.htm

Stillman College
P.O. Box 1430
Tuscaloosa, Alabama 35403
(205) 366-8817 or (800) 841-5722
www.stillman.edu/

Talladega College
627 West Battle Street
Talladega, Alabama 35160
(256) 761-6235 or (800) 633-2440
www.talladega.edu

Tennessee State University
3500 John Merritt Boulevard
Nashville, Tennessee 37209-1561
(615) 963-5101
www.tnstate.edu

Texas College
2404 North Grand Avenue
Tyler, Texas 75712-4500
(903) 593-8311
www.texascollege.edu

Texas Southern University
3100 Cleburne Street
Houston, Texas 77004-9987
(713) 313-7071
www.tsu.edu

Tougaloo College
500 West County Line Road
Tougaloo, Mississippi 39174
(601) 977-7770
www.tougaloo.edu

Trenholm State Technical College
1225 Air Base Boulevard
Montgomery, Alabama 36108
(334) 832-9000
www.trenholmtech.cc.al.us

Tuskegee University
102 Old Administration Building
Tuskegee, Alabama 36088
(334) 727-8011 or (800) 622-6531
www.tuskegee.edu/

University of Arkansas at Pine Bluff
1200 North University Drive
Pine Bluff, Arkansas 71611
(870) 575-8492 or (800) 264-6585
www.uapb.edu

University of Maryland Eastern Shore
Backbone Road
Princess Anne, Maryland 21853
(410) 651-2200
www.umes.edu

University of Texas at El Paso
500 West University Avenue
El Paso, Texas 79968
(915) 747-5890
www.utep.edu

University of the District of Columbia
4200 Connecticut Avenue NW
Washington, District of Columbia 20008
(202) 274 - 5000
www.udc.edu

University of the Virgin Islands
#2 John Brewers Bay Charlotte Amalie
St. Thomas, Virgin Islands 00802-9990
(340) 776-9200
www.uvi.edu/pub-relations/uvi/home.html

Virginia State University
One Hayden Street
Box 9018
Petersburg, Virginia 23806
(804) 524-5902
www.vsu.edu

Virginia Union University
1500 North Lombardy Street
Richmond, Virginia 23220
(804) 257-5600
www.vuu.edu

Virginia University of Lynchburg
2058 Garfield Avenue
Lynchburg, Virginia 24501-6417
434-528-5276
www.vulonline.org

Voorhees College
P.O. Box 678
Denmark, South Carolina 29042
(803) 793-3351
www.voorhees.edu

West Virginia State College
P.O. Box 1000
Institute, West Virginia 25112-1000
(304) 766-3000 or (800) 987-2112
www.wvsc.edu

Wilberforce University
P.O. Box 1001,1055 N. Bickett Road
Wilberforce, Ohio 45384-1001
(937) 708-5721
www.wilberforce.edu

Wiley College
711 Wiley Avenue
Marshall, Texas 75670
(903) 927-3300 or (800) 658-6889
www.wileyc.edu

Winston-Salem State University
601 Martin Luther King Jr. Dr
Winston-Salem, North Carolina 27110
(336)750-2000
www.wssu.edu

Xavier University of Louisiana
1 Drexel Drive
New Orleans, Louisiana 70125-1098
(504) 486-7411
www.xula.edu

Part Six
Internships & Other Career Choices

Gone are the days of using interns as simple "go-fers". Students are seeking opportunities that will stimulate them and provide real experience. A good internship program will ensure the assignment of challenging projects and tasks. Effective assignments are coupled with adequate supervision so as to provide an information resource and to ensure interns are keeping pace. Many programs will have some additional projects available in case an intern successfully completes a project ahead of schedule. Also, whenever possible, the interns will be involved in organization events such as staff meetings and have opportunities for networking and informational interviewing with key personnel.

There are two ways to approach an internship – for payment or course credit. If you opt for a paid internship, you will find that intern wages vary. However, it is required by law that interns must be paid at least minimum wage if they do not meet criteria for a "learner/trainee". The criteria state that the training must be comparable to that given at a vocational school; the training must benefit the student; the student would not replace regular employees; the employer does not immediately benefit from the student's activities; there is not a promise of a job following the training; and both employer and student understand that no wages will be given for the training period. It is a good idea to research common wage ranges within your industry and geographic location. You may consider calling a career services office in your area, as many collect this information.

On the other hand, employers may not be required to pay minimum wage if the student is receiving course credit for their work. In summary, credit must be obtained; the employer must receive formal documentation from the intern's college or university stating the educational relevance of the internship; learning objectives must be clearly stated; no more than 50% of the intern's work should be the same as other employees; and the intern must be supervised by a staff member.

More often than not, internships will lead to permanent placement after graduation from college.

Top 32 Minority Internship Programs Listings

Not all students want to receive academic credit for an internship; and many colleges and universities do not require credit for internship experience. You may obtain more detailed information from your legal counsel or your Human Resources department. Here we've listed 32 of the top internship programs for African Americans.

Accenture Internship Program
Accenture offers internships in a number of cities and countries around the world. Usually lasting between 10 – 12 weeks, you may participate in client or internal engagements where information systems and business skills are fostered and combined to help organizations effectively apply technology for competitive advantage.
> Location: Various
> More Info: http://careers3.accenture.com/Careers/Global/career_options

Academy of Television Arts and Sciences Student Internship Program
Undergraduate college students. This program is designed to give students in-depth exposure to professional facilities and practices during an eight week summer period.
> Location: Los Angeles.
> Award: $4,000 stipend + $300 spending allowance
> Deadline: March 15
> Contact: 818-754-2800
> More Info: www.emmys.tv/foundation/internships.php

American College of Healthcare Executives Minority Internship Program
This three-month internship program will provide an opportunity for the intern to rotate through all major ACHE divisions, including Administration, Communications and Marketing, Education, Executive

Office, Finance, Health Administration Press, Management Information Systems, Membership, Regional Services, and Research and Development. The internship program's content will be developed around the intern's special interests as well as in response to organizational needs. Applicants must have completed one year of graduate studies in a healthcare or association management program at a university that is accredited by the regional accrediting association in the United States approved by the U.S. Department of Education or that holds membership in the Association of Universities and Colleges of Canada.

    Location: Chicago, IL
    Award: $17.61 per hour (not eligible for benefits)
    Deadline: December 1
    Contact: Human Resources, American College of Healthcare Executives, 1 N. Franklin St., Ste. 1700, Chicago, IL 60606-3424 / 312-424-9341
    More Info: www.hr-intern-fellow@ache.org

American Society of Newspaper Editors

This program is for minority high school seniors who are interested in the field of journalism. Paid summer internship for minority freshmen and sophomores at their hometown or nearby newspaper. Must have a minimum 2.5 GPA.

    Location: Hometown
    Award: $750 ($250 bonus if they complete the program
    Deadline: Contact for details
    Contact: 703-453-1122
    More Info: www.asne.org

BET Internship Program
The majority of internships here at BET are non-paid, but they afford you the opportunity to receive college credit. The Black Entertainment Television Internship Program allows students to receive first-hand knowledge of the rewards and challenges of working for a multi-faceted entertainment company such as BET. Students will learn about BET's long and short-term goals and objectives, as well as gain an introductory experience into both the corporate and television production arenas.

> **Location:** Washington, DC and New York, NY
> **Contact:** 202-608-2020
> **More Info:** www.bet.com/Community/BETInternshipProgram.htm

Central Intelligence Agency Undergraduate Scholar Program
This program is open to high school seniors who are either a member of an ethnic group or have a disability. Applicants must be U.S. citizens, at least 18 years old, achieved 1000 on the SAT or 21 on the ACT, have a high school GPA of at least 2.75, meet the same employment standards as permanent CIA employees, and be able to demonstrate financial need. Applicant must also plan to major in computer science, economics, electrical engineering, foreign area studies, or non-Romance foreign languages. Recipients must be available to work for at least 90 calendar days each summer while in college.

> **Location:** Washington, D.C.
> **Award:** Interns receive an annual salary and up to $15,000 a year for tuition, fees, books and supplies. Summer travel to Washington, DC and a housing allowance while there are also provided.
> **Deadline:** June 1
> **Contact:** 800-368-3886
> **More Info:** CIA, Personnel Representative, POB 12727, Arlington, VA 22209

Congressional Black Caucus Foundation
Summer internship. Undergraduate students, a nine-month fellowship for graduate students interested on Public Policy. The CBCF also offers the Congressional Black Spouse Scholarship for undergraduates.

> **Location:** Contact for details.
> **Award:** Contact for details.
> **Deadline:** Contact for details.
> **Contact:** 202-675-6730
> **More Info:** www.cbcfonline.org

Congressional Youth Leadership Council

Applicant must be an undergraduate student and have a strong interest in political science, public policy and education. Duration: 4 months. Interns work from 20 to 40 hours per week; scheduling is generally flexible. Academic credit can be arranged with your school.

Location: Contact for details.
Award: All interns are paid a stipend of $9.00 per hour.
Deadline: March, August 30 and November
Contact: 202-777-4050
More Info: www.cycl.org

Global Service Corps Tanzania Internship Program

The Tanzania Internship Program is designed for those interested in an international development project learning experience who may also be considering an international career. This program is open to both students and adults. Interns have the unique opportunity to live with a local Tanzanian family while working on HIV/AIDS Prevention and Care or Sustainable Agriculture development projects. Internships consist of the core short-term program plus long-term extensions. GSC also offers an International Health Internship Program in Tanzania for pre-med and medical students, as well as health professionals.

Location: Tanzania, Africa
Contact: 415-788-3666
More Info: www.globalservicecorps.org/d/levelsTZintern.html

IBM Extreme Blue Internship

The Extreme Blue program is IBM's premier internship for top-notch students pursuing software development and MBA degrees. If you're chosen for the program, you become part of a team working in one of a dozen Extreme Blue labs around the world.

Location: Varies
Award: Varies
Deadline: February
Contact: extremeblue@info.ibm.com
More Info: www-913.ibm.com/employment/us/extremeblue/

Jackie Joyner-Kersee/Minority Internship

This internship provides women of color an opportunity to gain experience in a sports-related career and interact in the sports community. Internships are located at the Women's Sports Foundation in East Meadow, N.Y. The Women's Sports Foundation is a charitable educational organization dedicated to ensuring equal access to participation and leadership opportunities for all girls and women in sports and fitness. The Foundation's Participation, Education, Advocacy, Research and Leadership programs are made possible by individual and corporate contributions.

> **Location:** East Meadow, NY
> **Contact:** 516-542-4700
> **More Info:** www.cwu.edu/~scholar/outside/ womenssportsfoundation jackiejoyner.html

Kaiser Media Internships in Urban Health Reporting

This program is for minority, graduating journalism students. Focus: Health reporting.

> **Location:** National
> **Award:** $6,000 (minimum)
> **Deadline:** December
> **Contact:** 650-854-9400
> **More Info:** www.kff.org

Louis Carr Internship Foundation Paid Summer Internships In Communications

This non-profit foundation was organized to increase multiculturalism and promote diversity in the communications industry. They sponsor paid summer internships for minority college students during the summers following their sophomore or junior year in college. The LCIF believes that by enabling college students to experience a quality summer internship in the early stages of their careers, it will assist them to function more effectively in the corporate environment and encourage businesses in the communications industry to recruit, retain and promote a more diverse workforce.

> **Location:** Chicago, IL
> **Contact:** 800-524-3740
> **More Info:** www.louiscarrfoundation.com

Los Angeles Times Editorial Internships

Undergraduate or current graduate student in the communications field interested in doing an internship in any of the following: business, news and sports reporting, photo journalism and in copy editing and infographics. Summer positions are full time for 11 and 12 weeks. Spring and fall positions are about 24 hours a week. College credit available.

> **Location:** Los Angeles, CA
> **Award:** Contact for details
> **Deadline:** Contact for details
> **Contact:** 800-283-6397
> **More Info:** www.latimes.com

Minority Advertising Intern Program

Minority undergraduate and graduate students who have an interest in the field of communications. This program gives students a realistic view of what advertising is about by placing them in working environments.

> **Location:** Call for details.
> **Award:** $250/week
> **Deadline:** January 28
> **Contact:** 212-682-2500
> **More Info:** www.thephillipsfoundation.org

Minority Engineering Scholarship Program

This program is for African American students attending the University of Tennessee with a minimum GPA of 3.0, SAT of 940 and 3.5 units in mathematics.

> **Location:** Call for details.
> **Award:** $11,000 stipend guaranteed and co-op position with a major company
> **Deadline:** November 1
> **Contact:** 615-974-4457
> **More Info:** 325 Waukegan Road, Northfield, IL 60093-2750

NAHP – Presidential Classroom Scholars Program

This program is available to high school juniors and seniors with a minimum 3.8 GPA and an interest in Civic Education.

> **Location:** Call for details.
> **Award:** $100 - $500 stipend, and travel expenses for a one-week program in public policy and education.
> **Deadline:** April
> **Contact:** 800-441-6533
> **More Info:** www.presidentialclassroom.org

National Association of Black Journalists Scholarship and Internship

Black high school seniors, undergraduates, or graduate students majoring in print journalism, photography, radio or television, or are planning a career in one of those fields. The internship is open to undergraduate students who are completing their sophomore or junior year. Applicants must be majoring in print or broadcast journalism or planning a career in the communication field.

Location: Contact for details.
Award: Contact for details.
Deadline: Contact for details.
Contact: 301-445-7100
More Info: www.nabi.org.orghmtc

National Broadcasting Company (NBC) Corporate Internship

Incoming College students or current college students. Programs are designed to give students practical, on the job training and experience in the broadcast industry. Send a resume, cover letter and letter from your university stating you will get college credit for the internship.

Location: Contact for details.
Award: None
Deadline: Contact for details
Contact: 202-675-6730
More Info: www.cbcfonline.org

National Heart, Lung, and Blood Institute

Minority Summer Program in Pulmonary Research Program is intended to encourage qualified minority school faculty and graduate students to develop interest in skills in research in pulmonary diseases at established minority-pulmonary training centers.

Location: Contact for details.
Award: $733 per month
Deadline: August
Contact: 301-496-7668
More Info: http://grants.nih.gov/grants/guide/pa-files/PA-92-073.html

National Newspaper Publishers Association Scholarship and Intern Program
African American college students who are full-time juniors or seniors pursuing a career in journalism, Must have a 2.5 GPA.
> Location: Contact for details.
> Award: Contact for details
> Deadline: Contact for details
> Contact: 202-588-8764
> More Info: www.nnpa.org/news/default.asp

Proctor and Gamble Company
This internship is for minority students and provides opportunity for industrial research and product development.
> Location: Contact for details.
> Award: Salary and travel expenses
> Deadline: March 1
> Contact: 513-983-1100
> More Info: www.pg.com

Shell Legislative Internship Program
This internship is for an undergraduate college student of a 2 or 4-year institution and resident of AZ, CA, CO, FL, IL, NM, NY or TX of Latino origin. Need not attend college in these states. Participants are offered a summer of commitment to the Latino/a community. Must be a U.S. citizen or legal resident of Latino/a origin.
> Location: Contact for details.
> Award: $1,500
> Deadline: March 23
> Contact: 323-720-1932
> More Info: www.naleo.org

Summer Associates Program
This program is open to minorities, graduates interested in public affairs.
> Location: Contact for details.
> Award: $1,600 @ month for living expenses and $150 @ month for transportation expenses
> Deadline: April 15
> Contact: 415-284-7200
> More Info: www.greenlining.org

Summer Journalism Internship for Minorities
Minority undergraduate students completing their junior year and are interested in a career in journalism or mass communications. Starts in June.
　Location: Contact for details.
　Award: Tuition + $200 per week stipend
　Deadline: Contact for details
　Contact: 803-777-4104
　More Info: www.jour.sc.edu

Summer Programs in Biomedical Research
This program is for undergraduate students who wish to do a summer internship and acquire valuable hands on research training and experience in biomedical research or academic medicine. US citizen or resident. Must have a 3.0 GPA.
　Location: Contact for details.
　Award: Contact for details
　Deadline: March
　Contact: 301-496-5332
　More Info: www.ninds.nih.gov/eeo/summer.htm

Summer Research Program for Undergraduate Students
This program is open to undergraduate students focusing in science and biomedical science.
　Location: Contact for details.
　Award: $300 @ week
　Deadline: Late April
　Contact: 310-206-2182
　More Info: www.ucla.edu

The Dow Jones Newspaper Fund
For minority college sophomores and juniors; awards will include a paid summer internship to work at a daily newspaper.
　Location: Varies
　More Info: http://djnewspaperfund.dowjones.com/fund/

The Guy Hanks and Marvin Miller Screenwriting Program
This program was established by Drs. Bill and Camille Cosby in 1993, at the USC School of Cinema-Television. It was named in honor of Camille's father, Guy Alexander Hanks and Bill's producer, Marvin Miller. The fifteen-week intensive workshop was designed with a two-fold purpose: To assist writers in the completion of a film or television script; and, to deepen the participants' appreciation for and comprehension of African American history and culture. Up to fifteen participants will be chosen.
> **Location:** Los Angeles, CA
> **Contact:** 213-740-8194
> **More Info:** www.cosbyprogram.com

The INROADS Internship Program
The mission of INROADS is to develop and place talented minority youth in business and industry and prepare them for corporate and community leadership. INROADS seek high performing African American, Hispanic, and Native American students for internship opportunities with some of the nation's largest companies. Our rigorous career development training process will challenge you to commit to excellence and raise the bar on your personal expectations.
> **Location:** Varies
> **Contact:** 314-241-7488
> **More Info:** www.inroads.org/interns/internApply.jsp

TV One Internship Program
Interns at TV One, LLC receive hands-on education and training in the planning, coordination, and execution of a cable television network. Participants learn the day-to-day operations of programming, marketing, sales, accounting, legal, MIS, human resources or production. Our interns have a passion for the broadcast industry and are committed to their career development. Internship candidates must complete an Internship Application form and submit a one-page typed essay.
> **Location:** Washington, DC
> **Contact:** 301-755-0400
> **More Info:** www.tvoneonline.com/inside_tvone/careers.asp

Zora Neale Hurston/Richard Wright Foundation Summer Writing Workshop

This foundation is accepting applications for its annual Writers' Week summer workshop for Black writers. It is the nation's only multi-genre summer writer's workshop for writers of African descent with a tuition-free component for high school students. The workshop is held on the campus of American University in Washington, DC. Since the first workshop in the summer of 1996, over 700 writers have attended the week-long program of classes and presentations by publishers, agents and writers.

    Location: Washington, DC
    Contact: 301-683-2134
    More Info: www.hurston-wright.org/index.shtml

Popular Career Choices For African-Americans

The labor force is expected to hit nearly 155 million by the year 2008, and executive recruiters and career experts at historically Black colleges and universities say the best moves to make are the same time-honored moves that have worked for job-seekers over the past few years:

- Plan your job search.
- Prepare for your job search; and
- Network during your job search.

In planning your search, sit down with a list of jobs you will and will not do. Set aside two or three days out of the week to send out resumes and to go on interviews. When you've planned your job search, make sure you're prepared at every opportunity. Carry a couple of copies of your resume with you in clean, white envelopes and be prepared to give them to friends, relatives, and anyone else who can help you in your search. Network with those people who have the most to offer. Maybe some of their success can help you create your own!

For the most part, the best jobs and hottest fields remain a constant—engineering, computers, finance, health care. Find out what the strongest companies are in your desired field and gravitate toward those businesses. But you also have to look at the larger picture.

Entry-level salaries for positions such as linguists, engineers, biochemists and physicists range from $35,000 to $50,000, depending on your level of education. And, you should be eager and willing to go where the job takes you.

To help you in your career search, here is a list of the 10 top career choices for African-Americans.

Aides to Physical Therapists
Health care occupations comprise 10 out of 20 of the fastest-growing occupations based on a recent U.S. Labor Report.

Day Care Providers
Because there are more two-income families with young children, the demand for day care providers, both agency and in-home, will increase well into the next decade.

Computer Software Engineers
In a report by the U.S. Department of Labor, computer-related occupations accounted for 5 out of the 20 fastest-growing occupations. Growth estimates are based on businesses' increasing reliance on information technology, system security and network security businesses. Predictions include a greater demand for computer programmers, network and data analysts, and system technicians.

Dental Hygienists
Cosmetic dentistry and whitening procedures have sparked an increase in dental procedures, and accordingly, an increase in the need for dental hygienists. Providing chair-side assistance, the hygienist performs routine exams, procedures and prepares the patient for surgery and/or cosmetic procedures. They may also be responsible for admission policies, laboratory testing, X-ray requirements and patient education.

Home Health Aides
According to labor experts, the fastest-growing group of citizens will be seniors. Research suggests that the number of workers 55 and older is projected to increase 49.3 percent by 2012. This rise, and the corresponding needs of a larger and older population, will translate into an increased need for home health aides and related in-home health services.

Medical Assistants
The medical needs of an older population will require more assistants who provide administrative and procedural support to medical offices. Medical assistants are often responsible for patient in-take, record management, patient and staff scheduling, and other administrative tasks associated with the needs of the facility.

Nurses
Nurses and nurse educators are essential to meeting the medical needs of an older population.

Real Estate Appraisers
You cannot buy a home, or any other property, without the services of a real estate appraiser. Appraisals are also used for tax assessment, government acquisitions of private land, property disputes, estate evaluation and proposed business mergers.

Retail Salespersons
Because of the high rate of turnover in retail, there will be an ongoing demand for workers.

Teachers
The need for qualified teachers, teachers' aides and substitute teachers is increasing; especially in some inner-city neighborhoods, and more college students are considering teaching directly after graduation.

Post-Graduate Employment Opportunities

CarMax College Recruiting

If you're close to obtaining your Bachelor's Degree in Business, Engineering, Mathematics or another quantitative discipline, CarMax has some exciting opportunities waiting for you at an established and growing company in an exciting industry.

Location: Varies
More Info: www.carmax.com/ dyn/companyinfo/careers/
CollegeRecruiting.aspx

MasterCard Senior-Level Jobs

Today's winning companies hire and develop the best people they can find-smart, talented people who appreciate and understand unique customer needs, who connect with co-workers and customers, and who see the future in perceptive, innovative ways.

Location: Atlanta, GA; St. Louis, MO; Miami, FL; San Antonio, TX; San Ramon, CA and other cities.
More Info: http://sh.webhire. com/public/ 584/

Rockwell Collins Engineering Jobs

At Rockwell Collins, you can advance the future. You'll work with some of the most curious and innovative minds on the planet, shaping technology that shapes the world. We work hard to earn and keep our customers' trust. If you want to grow personally and professionally, we invite you to see if Rockwell Collins works for you.

Location: Varies
More Info: www.rockwellcollins .com/careers/ index.html

Part Seven

Exclusive Web Site Index Featuring The United Negro College Fund

Top Scholarships/Grants for African American Students

Accounting

American Institute of Certified Public Accountants Scholarships for Minority Accounting Students
http://http://www.aicpa.org/members/div/career/mini/smas.htm

John L. Carey Accounting Scholarship
http://www.aicpa.org/members/div/career/mini/jlcs.htm

Minorities in Government Finance Scholarship
http://www.gfoa.org

National Association of Black Accountants (NABA) Scholarship Program
http://www.nabainc.org/pages/Student_ScholarshipProgram.jsp

National Society of Accountants
http://www.nsacct.org

Actuary

Actuarial Scholarships for Minority Students
http://www.beanactuary.org/minority/scholarship.cfm

Agriculture

Booker T. Washington Scholarships
http://www.ffa.org

Architecture

American Institute of Architects/American Architectural Foundation
Foundation Minority Disadvantaged Scholarship Program
http://www.archfoundation.org

Association for Women in Architecture Scholarship
http://www.awala.org

Arts / Media

American Art Therapy Association Cay Drachnik Minorities Fund
http://www.arttherapy.org

Another Large Production Creative Excellence Scholarship
http://www.promax.tv/main.asp

Arts Recognition and Talent Search Scholarship Program
http://www.nfaa.org/Disciplines/index.htm

Chips Quinn Scholars Program For Journalism Students
http://www.chipsquinn.org/apply/index.aspx

Emma L. Bowen Foundation For Minority Interests In Media
http://www.emmabowenfoundation.com

Grants for Undergrads & Grads in Print and Television Photojournalism
http://www.nppa.org/professional_development/students/scholarships

Lagrant Foundation Scholarship
http://www.lagrantfoundation.org

MTV University Grants
http://www.mtvu.com/contests/mtvu_grants/details.jhtml

Music Assistance Fund Scholarship
http://www.sphinxmusic.org/programs/maf.html

National Association of Black Journalists Minority Scholarship
http://www.tennessean.com

National Association of Negro Musicians, Inc.
http://www.nanm.org/Scholarship_competition.htm

National Newspaper Publishers Scholarships
http://www.nnpa.org/News/default.asp

National Opera Association Vocal Competition/ Legacy Award Program
http://www.noa.org/voc.htm

Paul Zindel First Novel Award
http://www.hyperionbooksforchildren.com/contests.asp#zindel

Princess Grace Scholarships In Dance, Theater, and Film
http://www.pgfusa.com/awards/grants/index.html

Radio and Television News Directors Foundation Scholarships
http://www.rtnda.org/asfi/scholarships/undergrad.shtml

Ruben Salazar Memorial Scholarship
http://www.nahj.org

San Diego State University
http://www.sdsu.edu

Scholastic Art and Writing Awards
http://www.scholastic.com/artandwritingawards

SCRIPPS Howard Foundation Scholarships
http://foundation.scripps.com/foundation/programs/scholarships/scholarships.html

Student Journalist Impact Award
http://www.jea.org/awards/impact.html

The Editing Program
http://www.maynardje.org

The Freedom Forum
http://djnewspaperfund.dowjones.com/fund/

Corporate Scholarships / Programs

Armstrong World Industries, Inc.
http://www.armstrong.com

Bank of America: Financial Aid Sweepstakes
http://www.bankofamerica.com

Best Buy Scholarship Program
http://bestbuy.scholarshipamerica.org

Bonner Scholar Program
http://http://www.archfoundation.org

Coca-Cola Scholarship Award
http://www.coca-colascholars.org

College Prowler Essay Scholarship - Wachovia Monthly Scholarship
http://www.collegeprowler.com/the_scholarship.asp

Discover Card Tribute Award Scholarship Program
http://www.discoverfinancial.com/data/philanthropy/tribute.shtm

Duracell/National Urban League Scholarship
http://www.nul.org/scholarships.html

General Electric Foundation Engineering And Business Administration Scholarship Programs
http://www.ge.com/foundation/grant_initiatives/education/scholars.html

General Motors Minority Engineering and Science Scholarship (MES)
http://www.gm.com/company/careers/student/stu_scholar.html

Gillette/National Urban League Scholarship for Minority Students
http://www.nul.org/scholarships.html

Google Anita Borg Memorial Scholarship Program
http://www.groups.google.com/anitaborg

Intel Science Talent Search
http://www.sciserv.org/sts

Mercedes Benz "Drive Your Future" Scholarship Program
http://www.mbusa.com/drivefuture

Microsoft Computer Science Scholarships
http://www.microsoft.com/college/ss_howtoapply.mspx

Sears Craftsman Scholarship
http://www.nhra.com

State Farm Insurance National Merit Scholarship
http://www.statefarm.com/foundati/merit.htm

Tylenol Scholarship
http://scholarship.tylenol.com

Wal-Mart Scholarships
http://www.walmartfoundation.org

Wells Fargo Collegesteps Scholarship Program
http://www.wellsfargo.com/collegesteps

Xerox Technical Minority Scholarship Program
http://www.xerox.com/go/xrx/template/009.jsp?view=Feature&Xcntry=U
SA&Xlang=en_US&ed_name=Careers_Technical_Scholarship

Essays / Contests / Competitions

A. Patrick Charnon Scholarship
http://www.cesresources.org/charnon.html

AFSCME Family Scholarship
http://www.afscme.org/members/880.cfm

Applegate/Jackson/Parks Future Teacher Scholarship
http://www.nilrr.org/letter.htm

Atlas Shrugged Essay Contest
www.aynrand.org/site/PageServer?pagename=education_contests_atlas

aWorldConnected Essay Contest
http://www.aworldconnected.org/subcategory.php/311.html

Discovery Channel Young Scientist Challenge
http://school.discovery.com/sciencefaircentral/dysc/accept/accept.html

Elks National Foundation Most Valuable Student Contest
http://www.elks.org/enf/default.cfm

Ellen Masin Persina Scholarship
http://www.press.org

Ellie Wiesel Prize in Ethics Essay Contest
http://www.eliewieselfoundation.org

FBI Common Knowledge Challenge Scholarship Competition
www.cksf.org/index.cfm?Page=FindScholarships&Subpage=FBIProgram

Fountainhead Essay Contest
http://www.aynrand.org

Hispanic College Fund Scholarships
http://scholarships.hispanicfund.org

HIV/AIDS Story Writing Contest
http://www.hearmeproject.org

Mensa Education and Research Foundation Scholarship
http://www.merf.us.mensa.org

Michael J. Berkeley Foundation Golf Scholarship
http://www.mikebfoundation.org/scholarships.html

National Black Nurses Association
http://www.nbna.org/

National Fellowship of Black College Leaders Scholarship
http://www.hbcuconnect.com/NFBCL_Scholarship_Application1.pdf

Nelly's P.I.M.P (Positive. Intellectual. Motivated. Person) Scholarship Contest
http://www.letitloose.com

Siemens Westinghouse Scholarship Competition in Math, Science and Technology
http://www.siemens-foundation.org/competition

Society of Plastics Engineers "Wonder of Plastics" International Essay Contest
http://www.4spe.org/awards/essaycontest.php

Swackhamer Peace Essay Contest
http://www.wagingpeace.org

TechStudents.net Scholarship
http://www.techstudents.net/TechScholarship.asp

The Charles Shafae' Scholarship Fund
http://www.papercheck.com/scholarship.asp

The Collegiate Inventors Competition
http://www.invent.org/collegiate/overview.html

The "Dream Deferred" Essay Contest on Civil Rights
http://www.hamsaweb.org/essay-contest.php

The Dr. Robert Rufflo Scholarship Fund
http://www.metavue.com/Scholarships/mvcp_Scholarship.asp?id=4

The Olive W. Garvey Fellowship
http://www.independent.org/garvey.html

The Royce Osborn Minority Student Scholarship
http://www.asrt.org/content/ASRTFoundation/AwardsandScholarships/R
oyce_ Osborn.aspx

The Writer's Digest Annual Short Story Competition
http://www.writersdigest.com/contests/shortshort

Thomson Course Help Desk Scholarship Contest
http://www.course.com/helpdesk/rules.cfm

Voice of Democracy Scholarship Program, Veterans of Foreign Wars
http://www.vfw.org/yourtown/you_VoiceOf.htm

Writer's Digest Poetry Competition
http://www.writersdigest.com/contests/poetry/index.asp

Fellowships / Funds / Grants

Alice L. Haltom Educational Fund
http://www.alhef.org

American Association for the Advancement of Science
http://www.aaas.org

American Bar Foundation Fellowship Program ABF Summer Research Fellowships in Law & Social Science for Minority Undergraduate Students
http://www.abf-sociolegal.org/sumfel.html

American Geophysical Union
http://www.agu.org/sci/congress.fellow.html

American Hotel Foundation Hyatt Hotel Fund of Minority Lodging Management Students
http://www.hyatt.com/hyatt/about/diversity/community/hyatt-hotel-fun
d-for-minority.jsp

American Institute of Certified Public Accountants: Minority Fellowships
http://www.aicpa.org/members/div/career/mini/fmds.htm

American Planning Association Fellowship Program
http://www.planning.org/institutions/scholarship.htm#1

American Political Science Association Minority Fellows Program
http://www.apsanet.org/section_427.cfm

American Psychological Association Minority Fellowship Program
http://www.apa.org/mfp/hprogram.html

Fund for American Studies
http://www.tfas.org

Graduate Equity Fellowship Award
http://www.fullerton.edu

Harold W. Rosenthal Fellowship
http://www.rosenthalfellowship.org

Helen T. Carr Fellowship For HBCU Students
http://www.asee.org/resources/fellowships/hbecc.cfm

Institute of Current World Affairs
http://www.NIGMS.nih.gov

Institute of Industrial Engineers Scholarship and Fellowship Program
http://www.iienet2.org/Details.aspx?id=857

Jeanette Rankin Foundation Grants For Low-Income Women
http://www.rankinfoundation.org

Minority Leaders Fellowship Program
http://www.fsu.edu/~service/opp/sch_awards/sch_links.htm#minority

National Consortium for Graduate Degrees for Minorities in Engineering & Science, Inc.
http://www.gemfellowship.org

National Institute of General Medical Sciences
http://www.NIGMS.nih.gov

National Medical Fellowships, Inc.
http://www.nmf-online.org

National Science Foundation Fellowship
http://www.orau.org/nsf/nsffel.htm

Peace Scholar Dissertation Fellowship
http://www.usip.org/grants/index.html

Porter Physiology Fellowships for Minorities
http://www.the-aps.org/education/minority_prog/stu_fellows/porter_phy
/apInfo_pp.htm

Registered Nurse Fellowship Program For Ethnic/Racial Minorities
http://www.nursingworld.org/emfp/

Roothbert Fund
http://www.roothbertfund.org/scholarships.php#fund

Summer Undergraduate Research Fellowship in the Department of Pharmacology
http://www.uci.edu

The Davis-Putter Scholarship Fund
http://www.davisputter.org

The Stan Beck Fellowship
http://www.entfdn.org/BECK.html

The William Randolph Hearst Endowed Fellowship For Minority Students
http://www.nonprofitresearch.org/newsletter1530/newsletter_show.htm?
doc_id=16318

Foundations

Business and Professional Women's Foundation
http://www.bpwusa.org

Coca-Cola Scholars Foundation, Inc.
http://www.coca-colasholars.org

Educational Foundation of the National Restaurant Association
http://www.nraef.org

Foundation for Exceptional Children – Stanley E. Jackson Scholarship
http://www.yesican.sped.org

Future Leaders Program
http://www.thephillipsfoundation.org

Harry S. Truman Scholarship Foundation
http://www.truman.gov

World Study Foundation Scholarships
http://www.worldstudio.org

General Scholarship Programs

AGC Education and Research Foundation Undergraduate Scholarship
http://www2.agc.org/scholarship

American Institute of Real Estate Appraisers
/www.appraisalinstitute.org/education/downloads/Educ_Trst_Appl.pdf

American Library Association
http://www.ala.org

American Planning Association (3 scholarships)
http://www.planning.org

Alfred P. Sloan Foundation
http://www.sloan.org/main.shtml

Baptist Scholarship
http://www.nbcusa.org

Caribbean Tourism Organization Scholarship
www.onecaribbean.org/information/categorybrowse.php?categoryid=828

CIEE Education Abroad Scholarship Fund For Minority Students
http://www.ciee.org/study/scholarships.aspx

CLA Scholarship for Minority Students
http://www.cla-net.org/html/yelland.html

Cornell University Summer College Program, Jerome H. Holland Scholarships
http://www.summercollege.cornell.edu

Do Something BRICK Scholarships Awards
http://www.dosomething.org/awards/brick/apply

Dorothy Vandercook Peace Scholarship
http://www.grandmothersforpeace.org

Ecolab Scholarship Program
http://www.ahlef.org/scholarships_ecolab.asp

Education is Freedom National Scholarship
http://www.educationisfreedom.com

Excellence in Predicting the Future Award
http://www.cenimar.com/contest/award.jsp

Foundation For Exceptional Children Scholarships
http://www.cec.sped.org/student/

Girls Going Places Scholarship Program
http://www.girlsgoingplaces.com

Go On Girl Book Club Scholarships
http://www.goongirl.org/events/scholarship

Hallie Q. Brown Scholarship
http://www.nacwc.org/programs/scholarships.php

Harry S. Truman Scholarships
http://www.truman.gov/candidates/candidates_list.htm?cat_id=481

HBCU Study Abroad Scholarships
https://www.iesabroad.org/IES/Scholarships_and_Aid/financialAid.html

Horatio Alger Scholarship Program
http://www.horatioalger.com/scholarships/apply.cfm

Junior Summer Institute at the Woodrow Wilson School of Public and International Affairs, Princeton University
http://www.princeton.edu/jsi

National Association of Plumbing, Heating, and Cooling Contractors Education Foundation Scholarship
http://www.naphcc.org

National Association of Secondary School Principals – Principal Leadership Award
http://www.nassp.org

National Hispanic Scholarship Fund
http://www.hsf.net

National Merit Scholarship Corporation
http://www.nationalmerit.org

Sallie Mae Fund American Dream Scholarship
http://www.thesalliemaefund.org/smfnew/pdf/2007_Scholarship_Program-Fact_sheetBACK.pdf

Service Leadership Award
www.kaiserpermanente.org/locations/California/watts/watts-award.html

Special Libraries Association Affirmative Action Scholarship
www.sla.org/content/learn/scholarship/sch-index/index.cfm#aascholar

Stokes Educational Scholarship Program
http://www.nsa.gov/careers/students_4.cfm?#stokes

The Gates Millennium Scholarship Program
http://www.gmsp.org

The Ron Brown Scholar Program
http://www.ronbrown.org

The Tillie Golub-Schwartz Memorial Scholarship
www.localstudentfunding.org/content/scholarship.php?r=aag&sid=105

The U.S.A. Group Scholarship Program
http://www.sonoma.edu/cgi-bin/htsearch

The Women of Color Scholars Award at the University of Pennsylvania
http://www.upenn.edu/ccp/WOCAP/awards.html

Tri-Delta Undergraduate and Graduate Scholarships
http://www.tridelta.org/foundation/foundation_scholarships.asp

United States Senate Youth Program
http://www.hearstfdn.org/ussyp

William B. Ruggles Right To Work Scholarship
http://www.nilrr.org/ruggles1.htm

Healthcare Scholarships

ADA Endowment and Assistance Fund for Minority Dental Students
http://www.ada.org/ada/prod/adaf/prog_scholarship_prog.asp#minority

AHBAI
http://www.proudlady.org/scholar

AMBUCS Scholarship For Physical Therapists
http://www.ambucs.com/scholars/program_information.aspx

American Association of Women Dentists
http://www.womendentists.org

American Health and Beauty Aids Institute Fred Luster, Sr. Scholarships
http://www.ahbai.org/scholar/scholar_new.html

American Nurses Association Baccalaureate Completion Scholarship Program
http://www.nsna.org

American Respiratory Care Foundation
http://www.arcfoundation.org/awards/undergraduate/young.cfm

Breakthrough To Nursing Scholarship
http://college.enotes.com/scholarships-loans/foundation-national-studen
t-nurses-association#Breakthrough_to_Nursing_Scholarships_for_Racial
_Ethnic_Minorities

Ethnic Minority Bachelor's Scholarships
http://www.ons.org

Health Careers Opportunity Program Grants
http://bhpr.hrsa.gov/diversity/hcop/default.htm

Health Professionals Scholarship Program
http://www.ons.org

Indian Health Employees Scholarship Fund, Inc.
http://www.nmche.org

Minority Physical Therapist Professional Education Scholarships
http://www.ccapta.org

National Heart, Lung, and Blood Institute
http://grants.nih.gov/grants/guide/pa-files/PA-92-073.html

Nurses Educational Funds, Inc.
http://www.n-e-f.org/

The AORN Foundation Scholarship For Nursing Students
http://www.aorn.org/foundation/scholarships.asp

**The National Institutes of Health Minority Biomedical Research Support
Program**
http://www.nigms.nih.gov/Minority/MBRS/IMSDFAQ.htm#6

The National Institutes of Health Undergraduate Scholarship Program
http://www.ugsp.nih.gov/contact_us/contact_us.asp?m=10

Law

Justicia en Diversidad Scholarship Fund, Scholarship for high school students interested in Law
> http://www.law.harvard.edu/studorgs/alianza

Matt Garcia Memorial Scholarship
> http://www.maldef.org

The Earl Warren Legal Training, Inc.
> http://www.naacpldf.org/scholarships

Thurgood Marshall Scholarship Fund
> http://www.thurgoodmarshallfund.org

William Randolph Hearst Endowment scholarship
> http://www.maldef.org

Military

Air Force Society Grant
> http://www.afas.org

AMVETS National Headquarters
> http://www.afas.org

Army ROTC Four-Year Scholarship Program
> http://www.rotc.usaac.army.mil/scholarship_HPD2/fouryear/index.htm

United States Army Emergency Relief Scholarship
> http://www.aerhq.org/ArmyEmergencyRelief.htm

United States Marine Corps Scholarship Foundation
> http://www.marine-scholars.org

Science / Technology

Ace Ventures Web Design Scholarship
> http://www.acecarparts.com/scholarship.html

AHBAI
> http://www.aerhq.org/ArmyEmergencyRelief.htm

American Chemical Society/Minority Scholars Program
> http://www.chemistry.org

American Consulting Engineers Council Scholarship Program
http://www.acec.org

American Geological Institute, Minority Participation
http://www.agiweb.org/mpp/

American Meteorological Society
http://www.ametsoc.org/amsstudentinfo/scholfeldocs/index.html

American Nuclear Society (ANS) Undergraduate Scholarships
http://www.ans.org

American Physical Society
http://www.aps.org/programs/minorities/honors/scholarship/index.cfm

American Society of Civil Engineers
http://www.asce.org

American Society of Safety Engineers (ASSE) Foundation Scholarship Awards
http://www.asse.org/foundat.htm

American Society for Microbiology
http://www.asm.org/edusrc/edu23b.htm

Anchor Environmental Scholarship
http://www.anchorenv.com/Scholarship.htm

ASHRAE Engineering Scholarship Program
http://www.ashrae.org/students/page/747

Development Fund for Black Students in Science and Technology
http://ourworld.compuserve.com/homepages/dlhinson/dfb_sch.htm#
Obtaining_Appl

Earthwatch Expeditions Inc.
http://www.earthwatch.org/ed/scdurfee.html

Ethan and Allan Murphy Memorial Scholarship
http://www.asm.org/edusrc/edu23b.htm

Flipnut Innovations General Education Scholarship
http://www.flipnut.com/general/apply.php

Minority Geoscience Undergraduate Scholarships
http://www.agiweb.org

NAACP Scholarship Program
http://www.naacp.org/advocacy/education/

NAACP Willems Scholarship
http://www.naacp.org/advocacy/education/

NACME Scholarship Program
http://www.nacme.org/scholarships/

National Science Teachers Association
http://www.nsta.org

National Security Agency Undergraduate Training Program
/www.adventuresineducation.org/Scholarships/detail.cfm?ID=00431

National Society of Black Engineers Scholarships
http://www.nsbe.org/scholarships

Society of Women Engineers
http://www.swe.org/

Sororities / Fraternities

Alpha Kappa Alpha Educational Advancement Scholarship
http://www.akaeaf.org/scholarships.htm

Phi Beta Sigma Fraternity
http://admissions.boisestate.edu/afrischlr.shtml

Sports

AAU Youth Excel Program Scholarship, Amateur Athletic Union (AAU)
http://www.aausports.org

Dorothy Harris Endowed Scholarship
http://www.womenssportsfoundation.org/cgi-bin/iowa/funding/featured.
html?record=3

Ethnic Minority and Women's Enhancement Postgraduate Scholarship for
Careers in Athletics
http://www1.ncaa.org/membership/ed_outreach/prof_development/min
ority-womens_scholarships.html

Jackie Robinson Foundation Scholarship Fund
http://www.jackierobinson.org/apply/index.php

SAMMY Award
http://www.whymilk.com

USBC Bowling Scholarships For Young Bowlers
http://www.bowl.com/scholarships/main.aspx

Women's Sports Foundation
http://www.lifetimetv.com/WoSport

Top Minority Internships

Academy of Television Arts and Sciences Student Internship Program
http://www.emmys.tv/foundation/internships.php

American College of Healthcare Executives Minority Internship Program
http://www.hr-intern-fellow@ache.org

American Society of Newspaper Editors
http://www.asne.org

BET Internship Program
http://www.bet.com/Community/BETInternshipProgram.htm

Congressional Youth Leadership Council
http://www.cycl.org

Global Service Corps Tanzania Internship Program
http://www.globalservicecorps.org/d/levelsTZintern.html

Jackie Joyner-Kersee/Minority Internship
http://www.cwu.edu/~scholar/outside/womenssportsoundation
jackiejoyner.html

Kaiser Media Internships in Urban Health Reporting
http://www.kff.org

Louis Carr Internship Foundation Paid Summer Internships In Communications
http://www.louiscarrfoundation.com

Minority Access Internship Program
http://www.minorityaccess.org/intern_student_info_04.htm

Minority Advertising Intern Program
http://www.thephillipsfoundation.org

National Heart, Lung, and Blood Institute
http://grants.nih.gov/grants/guide/pa-files/PA-92-073.html

NAHP – Presidential Classroom Scholars Program
http://www.presidentialclassroom.org

Proctor and Gamble Company
http://www.pg.com

Shell Legislative Internship Program
http://www.naleo.org

Summer Associates Program
http://www.greenlining.org

Summer Programs in Biomedical Research
http://www.ninds.nih.gov/eeo/summer.htm

Summer Research Program for Undergraduate Students
http://www.ucla.edu

The Dow Jones Newspaper Fund
http://djnewspaperfund.dowjones.com/fund/

The Guy Hanks and Marvin Miller Screenwriting Program
http://www.cosbyprogram.com

The INROADS Internship Program
http://www.inroads.org/interns/internApply.jsp

TV One Internship Program
http://www.tvoneonline.com/inside_tvone/careers.asp

Zora Neale Hurston/Richard Wright Foundation Summer Writing Workshop
http://www.hurston-wright.org/index.shtml

Scholarship Gateways/Portals & Aid Resources

Aid & Resources For Re-Entry Students
More Info: http://wwwback2college.com/

Black Alliance for Educational Options Scholarships (preschool - 12th grade students to attend private schools)
More Info: http://www.baeo.org/resources

BOEING scholarships (some HBCU connects)
More Info:
http://search-www2.boeing.com/search?q=Scholarship&site=www_boeing&client=www_boeing&proxystylesheet=www_boeing&output=xml_no_dtd&btnG.x=3&btnG.y=6

College Board Scholarship Search
More Info:
http://cbweb10pcollegeboard.org/fundfinder/html/fundfind01.html

CollegeNet 's Scholarship Database
More Info: http://mach25.collegenet.com/cgi-bin/M25/index

Ed Finance Group Scholarship Links
More Info: http://www.efg.net/link_scholarship.htm

FAFSA On The Web (Your Key Aid Form & Info)
More Info: http://www.fafsaed.gov/

Federal Scholarships & Aid Gateways 25 Scholarship Gateways from Black Excel
More Info: http://www.blackexcel.org/25scholarships.htm

FinAid: The Smart Students Guide to Financial Aid scholarships
More Info: http://www.finaid.org/

Graduate Fellowships For Minorities Nationwide
More Info:
http://cuinfo.cornell.edu/Student/GRFN/list.phtml?category=MINORITIES

Guaranteed Scholarships
More Info: http://www.guaranteed-scholarships.com/

Historically Black College & University Scholarships
More Info: http://www.iesabroad.org/info/hbcu.htm

Instituteforbrandleadership (gateway)
More Info: http://instituteforbrandleadership.org/

International Students Scholarships & Aid Help
    More Info: http://www.iefa.org/

Minority Scholar Resources - American Political Science Association -
    More Info: http://www.apsanet.org/PS/grants/aspen3.cfm

Multiple List of Minority Scholarships
    More Info:
    http://gehon.ir.miami.edu/financial-assistance/Scholarship/black.html

Scholarship & Financial Aid Help
    More Info: http://www.blackexcel.org/fin-sch.htm

ScienceNet Scholarship Listing
    More Info:
    http://www.sciencenet.emory.edu/undergrad/scholarships.html

Scholarships and Fellowships Opportunities
    More Info: http://www.osc.cuny.edu/sep/link%20s.html
    Plus: http://ccmi.uchicago.edu/schl1.html

The PhD Project: Business Doctoral Programs For Minorities
    More Info: http://www.phdproject.org

Union Sponsored Scholarships and Aid
    More Info: http://www.aflcioorg/scholarships/scholar.htm

WiredScholar Free Scholarship Search
    More Info:
    www.wiredscholar.com/paying/scholarship_search/pay_scholarship%20_
    search.jsp

United Negro College Fund

About UNCF

The United Negro College Fund (UNCF) is the nation's largest, oldest, most successful and most comprehensive minority higher education assistance organization. UNCF provides operating funds and technology enhancement services for 39 member historically black colleges and universities (HBCUs), scholarships and internships for students at about 900 institutions and faculty and administrative professional training.

Over 63 years, the United Negro College Fund has raised more than $2 billion to help a total of more than 350,000 students attend college and has distributed more funds to help minorities attend school than any entity outside of the government.

UNCF at 63

- Today, of the approximately 65,000 students UNCF supports at about 900 colleges and universities, some 60% are the first in their families to attend college and 62% have annual family incomes of less than $25,000.

- UNCF provides operating support to 39 member historically black colleges and universities (HBCUs), which helps the member schools keep tuition down to a rate 54% lower than tuition at other comparable schools.

- UNCF administers more than 400 scholarships and fellowships that support students at the undergraduate, graduate and doctoral level.

- Hundreds of students participate in UNCF Corporate Scholars programs, which provide scholarships and internships with major Fortune 500 corporations.

- UNCF Liberty Scholarships enable children of the victims of the September 11th terrorist attacks- regardless of age, race, creed or color, to attend any UNCF member institution.

- Targeted UNCF programs support post-doctoral bioscience and biotechnology research.

- The UNCF-administered Gates Millennium Scholars program, funded through one of the largest charitable gifts in history, can support a student from undergraduate school through their doctoral education.

- UNCF administers tens of millions of dollars that help provide computers, technology integration training for faculty members and technological infrastructure support for HBCUs.

History of UNCF

In 1943, Dr. Frederick D. Patterson, president of what is now Tuskegee University, urged his fellow black college presidents to raise money collectively through an "appeal to the national conscience." The next year, on April 25, 1944, Dr. Patterson, Dr. Mary McLeod Bethune and others incorporated the United Negro College Fund) with 27 member colleges. Early supporters included President Franklin Delano Roosevelt and John D. Rockefeller, Jr. Later, then Senator John F. Kennedy donated the proceeds from his Pulitzer Prize winning book, *Profiles in Courage* to UNCF.

Ad agency Young and Rubicam executive Forest Long created the UNCF tagline "A mind is a terrible thing to waste," in 1972 as a "plea to everybody to reject the prejudices of the past and consider the inner person." It is one of the most recognized slogans in advertising history. The award-winning UNCF ad campaigns featuring the tagline have attracted hundreds of millions of dollars in donated advertising support and have included such notable figures as Spike Lee, Jr., Michael Jordan and President George H.W. Bush.

Hundreds of thousands of individuals have become part of the UNCF family through volunteering and donating resources. One of UNCF's signature events, *The Lou Rawls Parade of Stars/An Evening of Stars* has raised over $200 million for UNCF students and has featured some of the world's most extraordinary talent and celebrities, including Bill Cosby, Whitney Houston, Beyonce, Stevie Wonder, Frank Sinatra, Debbie Allen, Sammie Davis, Jr., Harry Belafonte, Usher, Boyz II Men, Mariah Carey, Diahann Caroll, Ed McMahon, Chaka Khan, New Edition, Oprah Winfrey, Lauryn Hill, Richard Pryor, President Ronald Reagan, the Winans and many, many more.

Graduates of UNCF institutions have made lasting contributions to our nation by building successful careers in the fields of business, politics, health care and the arts, to name a few. Some prominent UNCF alumni include:

- Dr. Martin Luther King, Jr.- Nobel Laureate and civil rights leader
- The Honorable Alexis Herman- former U.S. Secretary of Labor
- Spike Lee- director, actor
- Samuel L. Jackson- actor
- General Chappie James- the U.S. Air Force's first African American four-star general
- Dr. David Satcher- former U.S. Surgeon General and former director, Centers for Disease Control and Prevention
- Dr. Walter Massey, former director, National Science Foundation, and president, Morehouse College
- Dr. Ruth Simmons- president of Brown University and first African American president of an Ivy League school
- The Honorable Hazel O'Leary- former U.S. Secretary of Energy
- Dr. Deborah Hyde- one of only four African American female neurosurgeons in the United States
- The Honorable Louis Sullivan- former U.S. Secretary of Health and Human Services
- Dr. Leroy T. Walker- former president, U.S. Olympic Committee
- Ellis Marsalis- jazz musician; patriarch of talented Marsalis music family
- Carl Ware- former Coca-Cola senior vice president
- Dr. W.E.B. DuBois- writer, scholar educator
- Willie Gary- prominent lawyer
- Dr. Marian Wright Edelman- founder and president, Children's Defense Fund
- Lionel Ritchie- singer

- The Honorable L. Douglas Wilder- 1 st African American governor to be elected
- Keisha Knight-Pulliam- actress
- Randall Robinson- founder of TransAfrica
- Rev. Dr. Floyd Flake- president of Wilberforce University and former Congressman
- James Farmer- civil rights leader
- Tom Joyner- radio personality
- U.S. Representative Sanford Bishop (GA)
- U.S. Representative Alcee Hastings (FL)
- U.S. Representative John Lewis (GA)
- U.S. Representative Major Owens (NY)
- U.S. Representative Bennie Thompson (MS)

Access to a college education has never been more important for individuals and society! A college education opens up unlimited possibilities and helps students to discover and foster their unique gifts. It also demonstrates that students are willing to make an investment in their own futures. However, for many young people this investment cannot become a reality, because they are unable to afford the rising cost of college tuition.

Since 1985, the UNCF Scholarships and Grants Administration office has awarded in scholarship assistance over $105 million to over 28,000 students enrolled in its 39 member colleges and universities and other HBCUs and majority institutions as well. We provide support in numerous ways to a variety of constituencies:

<u>Students:</u> Scholarships that pay for tuition, room and board, and any mandatory fees associated with direct educational costs. Opportunities through internships with corporations throughout the United States are also available to provide valuable hands-on experience to assist in career development of our students.

<u>Member Colleges/Universities:</u> Funding to our member institutions in order to maintain low tuition cost and nurturing environments. Grants also provide needed assistance to help building capacity of the UNCF network.

<u>Faculty Development:</u> Grants to enhance teacher training among UNCF faculty members.

Scholarships and faculty development grants administered by the UNCF are intended to facilitate access to UNCF member institutions and to strengthen the quality of education that these colleges and universities offer. You can use the UNCF site to search through hundreds of scholarship and grant programs administered by the United Negro College Fund. You will have access to both **UNCF SCHOLARSHIPS** and scholarships administered by many other organizations. As you search, you can apply online for any of the UNCF scholarships.

If you are a student attending a UNCF member college or university, it is highly recommended that you complete the **Uncf General Scholarship** application. Once a student completes a UNCF General Scholarship application, the information will be used to match you to many of the specific programs administered by UNCF. Should additional information be needed to complete your application for another UNCF scholarship, our online process with alert you of the additional information required to complete your application.

If you have been selected for a UNCF scholarship, students will receive an official award letter from UNCF. Students can also check the status of their application by logging onto the UNCF website and going to their individual Home Page.

Internships

UNCF Corporate Scholars
Money for college, experience for a lifetime!

UNCF Corporate Scholars Programs help college students gain invaluable professional experience through paid internships at America's leading Fortune 500 corporations and national organizations. Students also receive up to a $10,000 scholarship. Many of the internships are renewable. The ultimate goal of the program is to ensure that successful corporations have a ready pool of well-trained, ethnically diverse young professionals who can create the products and efficiencies companies need to compete in the dynamic, globally integrated marketplace of today. Eligibility requirements are different for each program. Hundreds of students have participated in the program, resulting in money for college and abundant job offers.

The Corporate Scholars Program gives their corporate partners an advantage over other companies seeking to recruit the best talent for their workforce. UNCF has demonstrated an unparalleled ability to reach the nation's most competent college students, including use of a unique network of on-campus placement, academic and financial faculty contacts that can get information to the right applicant quickly and efficiently. They tailor integrated marketing plans to increase awareness of internship opportunities through print, electronic and other visual media. UNCF also employs a technologically state of the art process of professional screening to find applicants who meet the corporation's criteria for acceptable interns. Adding the historic credibility of UNCF to a company's recruiting efforts increases exponentially their ability to employ exactly the kind of college graduate needed to increase their talent pool.

The UNCF Corporate Scholars Program is a turnkey solution for both students and employers seeking to find the right professional match. The following are among the participating corporations:

- Booz/Allen/Hamilton
- Catholic Healthcare West
- Dell
- Ford

- HSBC
- JP Morgan Chase
- Malcolm Pirnie
- Marathon Oil Company
- Oracle
- Pepsico
- Pfizer
- Rockwell Automation
- Sprint
- UPS
- Weyerhaeuser

Students applying for an internship can go to the UNCF website and either select a program from the toolbar or see an overview of all programs and requirements.

For more information about the Internships offered, contact:

UNCF Corporate Scholars Program
8260 Willow Oaks Corporate Drive
Fairfax, VA 22031
Phone: 1-866-671-7237
Email: internship@uncf.org

Fellowships

Research is an important part of both the academic and corporate environments, and minorities play a critical role in scientific advancement. United Negro College Fund funded more than 300 research fellowships at the postdoctoral, pre-doctoral and undergraduate levels to increase the exposure of minorities to research fields and to help researchers identify talented professionals who can lend their expertise to scientific and other research endeavors. UNCF also recognizes the critical importance of research to faculty development, and administers a number of programs designed to help minority professors increase their research experience. UNCF fellows make a real contribution to the collective advancement of humanity through unique discoveries.

Exposure to research and development fellowships significantly increase a student or professional's ability to relate theoretical knowledge with hands-on activity. It enhances the entire learning atmosphere, as the experience is integrated into curricula or communicated among peers. It gives greater relevance to classroom instruction, and ensures that the latest academic theory is transplanted into the research arena. It also increases the pool of potential PhDs., who can then lend their expertise to classroom instruction.

For more information, contact:

UNCF Fellowships
8260 Willow Oaks Corporate Drive
Fairfax, VA 22031
Phone: 1-800-331-2244

How To Have A Successful College Experience

College Survival Tips

You've made it! Now here are some tips to help you survive and thrive during your freshman year—and throughout your college career.

Don't miss class!
Study more and party less than you want to! Strike a balance between studying and social life.

Remain focused.
This may be your first time on your own, and you may find yourself tempted by many distractions. However, it's important to never forget why you're at school.

Although you may not want to admit it to anyone, including yourself, you might be a little nervous and a little scared. That's ok. Take that nervous energy and use it to push yourself to make new friends:

- Find a sophomore, junior or senior mentor (someone with your same major, someone from your same state, a friend of a friend., etc.)

- Get to know the campus like the back of your hand;

- Get to know your professors and your counselor; and

- Get to know people at your dorm.

However, don't be so eager to be accepted by others that you cause problems for you (i.e **don't lend** money/clothes/food, etc. *until you have none*). **Watch** and observe others, then use common sense and make wise friendship choices.

Register for classes early!
Don't schedule classes earlier or later than you know you can handle (i.e. if you're not an early bird, don't sign up for an 8:00 a.m. class (unless you have no other choice).

Be sure and get all the books you need for each class. No matter how long the bookstore line is—be patient. You might also be able to save money by getting used books.

Get involved in extracurricular activities and clubs.
This will help you build your leadership capabilities and will give you the chance to learn a lot from others who can share the benefit of their experience with you.

STUDY, STUDY, STUDY on a daily basis, take a break, AND STUDY MORE.

While your friends are hanging out at the student center, playing cards or just shooting the breeze, **you should be studying.** You can hone your social skills at the party later that evening, after you've completed your studies.

Take notes on everything your instructor says. No matter how insignificant you may think it is. Then re-write your notes to put them more indelibly in your mind. If you are not good at taking notes, then use a tape recorder. Copy down your notes as you listen to them on tape.

There is no such thing as a stupid question. Don't hesitate to ask your questions before, during or after class. Establish a connection with your professor. Let the professor know that you want to succeed in class. Make an appointment to speak with the professor or his or her teaching assistant if you have a special concern. If you have a question about your grade, don't be afraid to ask for an explanation. Your professor really would like to see you do well. You may even end up with a mentor.

The more a student achieves, the more effective the professor thinks he or she is. If he or she sees you taking a special interest in the course, the professor will most likely take a special interest in your success!

Be prepared before class. Read all of the chapters that your instructor suggests you read. College instructors often give impromptu quizzes.

Go to class yourself! Some students skip classes thinking they can catch up by reading the book or getting the notes from another student. **DO NOT MAKE THAT MISTAKE.** Don't trust someone else's notes to give you everything you need. They probably will miss exactly what you need to hear. Besides, how can you trust your future in anyone's hands but yours?

DO IT NOW WHILE YOU HAVE THE OPPORTUNITY.

There is no room in your life for procrastination if you want to succeed in college. Get it done while you can, while your mind is fresh. Then you can enjoy yourself with a clear conscience once you have your studies done.

What if you hit a brick wall and can't study a moment longer? Then go out and do something that you really enjoy. Partake in some intense fun. Then go back refreshed to your studies.

Yes, all work and no play will make you very dull. Therefore, take some time for you.

- There are a lot of interesting people at your university.
- Enjoy their company.
- Take time to get to know your fellow students.
- Get involved in the community life at your college.
- Have a great time.

College is wonderful! Your college years will be one of the best times of your life.

Remember, balance is the key. In the final analysis, you came to college to get a degree. You didn't go there to be elected your university's social director. However, you can succeed academically and have fun as well. There are campus queens who have graduated summa cum laude and star athletes who have graduated phi beta kappa. Put forth your full effort, and soak up the college experience to achieve your personal best.

Take care of yourself. Now your mom won't be there to nag you about healthy eating habits, but mom really knows what she's talking about. While you're in pursuit of independence, don't neglect yourself. Be sure to get the proper food, rest and exercise that your body needs.

Nurture your mind and spirit with the things that enhance your thoughts and make your soul sing. Put a lid on stress with stress reduction activities. You may want to:

- Go to a campus film fest.
- Dance 'til you drop.
- Sing with the campus choir.
- Go watch a ball game.
- Get involved in sports; or
- Meet your friends to talk things over.

If you feel you need special attention, **call the campus hotline or make an appointment to talk with a counselor.** There's usually a solution to every challenge if you keep looking for it. Whatever is on your mind, **don't give up** until you find an answer.

Handle your finances. College may be the first time that you've had to be fully responsible for managing your finances. Don't panic. Just stay on top of the situation. You most likely will need to open a checking account to keep track of your bills.

- Be sure to write down everything in your checkbook
- Keep your account balanced.
- Keep good records of your expenditures
- Make a budget and do your best to stick to it.

You don't want to run out of money. You don't want any surprises with having less money than you thought you had.

You may find that you are such a good money manager that other students start coming to you to borrow. Lending your friends money is really **not a good idea unless you can afford not to be paid back.** Things may come up and your friends may not repay you. You'll be out of money and have a strained friendship. Unless your friends have dire circumstances or the amount is very small, it's best to let them know that **you just can't give them a loan.** If the person is really your friend, he or she will appreciate your forthright answer.

Living with a roommate. You might think your roommate walks on water. Or you may get a roommate who wants to play his or her saxophone at 3:00 in the morning. Most likely you'll get someone between those extremes. What's the best way to live with a roommate?

- Respect his or her time and space.

- Be tolerant.

- Be friendly and maybe you'll end up with a friend for life. You may find that you'll prefer having a roommate all four years of your college. Or you may find that it's best if you live in a dorm room alone. Either way:

- Be true to yourself, and do what is best for you.

Relationships with others. In college you're going to meet a wide variety of people from diverse backgrounds. Take the opportunity to get to know as many people as you can. Some of the friends you make in college you'll keep for a lifetime. Even if some of the people whom you meet in college rub you the wrong way, they've given you the opportunity for growth.

Everybody can be an example—some are good examples, some are bad ones. Keep an open mind with people. Now is your time to learn as much as possible as you continue to develop who you are.

Of course romance is in the air when you get to college. You're bound to meet many people whom you will find physically and intellectually attractive, so consider these points:

- Keep your head clear.

- Take it slow.

- Don't rush into anything you may later regret.

- Don't let anyone pressure you. They don't have to live in your skin, you do.

- Make sure you're comfortable in your choices.

- Develop a relationship with someone who is worthy of your time and who appreciates you and your unique qualities.

- Take the time to get to know as many individuals as you can on a friendship basis. This learning process of what makes others tick will help give you the knowledge to make good friendship basis. This learning process of what makes others tick will help give you the knowledge to make good choices.

Greek Letter Organizations. Most likely, your campus will have fraternities or sororities that you may want to consider joining. There is a special bond among members of these sisterhoods and brotherhoods that extends into the world of careers. Perhaps a relative is a member of a Greek letter organization that you've always admired. Maybe you have friends who want you to join them in the organization. If you should decide to join a Greek letter organization you should:

- Fully contemplate what its ideals and goals are.
- Look to see if its community service goes beyond just words;
- Find out if it is really put into action.

You should be a part of an organization that means something. You may decide you do not wish to join one of these organizations. You may feel perfectly happy with retaining your status as an individual — choosing instead to pledge "me phi me." Again, do what's right for you. You don't have to please or impress anyone but yourself.

Believe in Yourself

Go to college believing that you can achieve a straight A average. Believe that you can graduate phi beta kappa or summa cum laude. For example,

One historically Black college graduate read the university handbook in her freshman year. It stated that one could graduate summa cum laude with a grade point average of 3.9 or above (out of 4.0). She made up her mind that was what she would do. Although she ended up with a grade point average of 3.85 and graduated magna cum laude, she still had made a major accomplishment. It turned out that graduating magna cum laude from her prestigious university held as much weight with employers as a master's degree. It showed potential employers that she was an achiever. The graduate found out that even though she reached for the moon, she landed upon the stars.

After you believe that you can achieve, you have to put forth the effort. *You can do the same, or better, with the proper mind-set.*

About Dante Lee

Dante Lee is the president and CEO of Diversity City Media, a very successful multicultural marketing and public relations firm based in Columbus, Ohio. His company produces BlackNews.com, an online African American newspaper; BlackPR.com, a press release distribution service to the Black media; and BlackStudents.com, a free resource for students looking for scholarships and internships. The company has a staff of five, annual billings of about $500,000, and big-name clients including: Verizon, McDonald's, NASCAR, BET, and Nationwide Insurance.

Lee was recently recognized as one of the "Top 30 Young Leaders For 2006" by *Ebony Magazine,* and was nominated for the 2006 Small Business of the Year Award by *Black Enterprise Magazine.* He has been featured as a panelist at the Tavis Smiley Leadership Institute in Houston, and was the keynote speaker at the AT&T Black Telecommunications Conference in St. Louis.

Dante earned a Bachelor's degree in Computer Science from Bowie State University, and was the only student in the school's 100-year history to graduate from a 4-year program in three years.

Dante is a self-taught pianist, a motivational speaker, and the author of *How To Think Big…When You're Small.*

ORDER FORM

WWW.AMBERBOOKS.COM
African-American Self Help and Career Books

Fax Orders: 480-283-0991
Telephone Orders: 480-460-1660
Online Orders: E-mail: Amberbks@aol.com

Postal Orders: Send Checks & Money Orders to:
Amber Books Publishing
1334 E. Chandler Blvd., Suite 5-D67, Phoenix, AZ 85048

____ *The African-American Family's Guide to Tracing Our Roots* $14.95
____ *Literary Divas: The Top 100+ Most Admired African American Women in Literature* $16.95
____ *Beside Every Great Man…Is A Great Woman* $14.95
____ *How to Be an Entrepreneur and Keep Your Sanity* $14.95
____ *Real Estate and Wealth…Investing in the American Dream* $15.95
____ *The African-American Writer's Guide to Successful Self-Publishing* $14.95
____ *Fighting for Your Life: The African American Criminal Justice System Survival Guide* $14.95
____ *Urban Suicide: The Enemy We Choose Not to See* $14.95
____ *How to Get Rich When You Ain't Got Nothing* $14.95
____ *The African-American Job Seeker's Guide to Successful Employment* $14.95
____ *The African-American Teenagers Guide to Personal Growth, Health, Safety, Sex and Survival* $19.95
____ *No Mistakes: The African-American Teen Guide to Growing Up Strong* $14.95
____ *Black Out: The Black Person's Guide to Redefining A Career Path Outside of Corporate America* $15.95
____ *2007-2009 African American Scholarship Guide for Students and Parents* $15.95

Name:_____

Company Name:_____

Address:_____

City:_____State:_____Zip:_____

Telephone: (____) _____E-mail:_____

Tracing Our Roots	$14.95	❏ Check ❏ Money Order ❏ Cashiers Check
Literary Divas	$16.95	❏ Credit Card: ❏ MC ❏ Visa ❏ Amex ❏ Discover
Beside Every Great Man	$14.95	
How to be an Entrepreneur	$14.95	CC#_____
Real Estate and Wealth	$15.95	
Successful Self-Publishing	$14.95	Expiration Date:_____
Fighting for Your Life	$14.95	
Urban Suicide	$14.95	**Payable to:** Amber Books
How to Get Rich	$14.95	1334 E. Chandler Blvd., Suite 5-D67
Job Seeker's Guide	$14.95	Phoenix, AZ 85048
Teenagers Guide	$19.95	
No Mistakes	$14.95	**Shipping:** $5.00 per book. Allow 7 days for delivery.
Black Out	$15.95	**Sales Tax:** Add 7.05% to books shipped to AZ addresses.
Scholarship Guide	$15.95	**Total enclosed: $_____**